The View from the Back of the Pulpit

The View from the Back of the Pulpit

J. Mark Jordan

The View from the Back of the Pulpit

Copyright © 2007
J. Mark Jordan

Unless otherwise identified, all Scripture quotations are from the King James Version of the Bible.
Scripture quotations marked NKJV taken from the New King James Version®, Copyright © 1982 by Thomas Nelson, Inc. Used by permission. All rights reserved.
Scripture quotations marked NIV are taken from the HOLY BIBLE, NEW INTERNATIONAL VERSION®. NIV®. Copyright © 1973, 1978, 1984 by International Bible Society. Used by permission of Zondervan Publishing House. All rights reserved.

ALL RIGHTS RESERVED
No portion of this publication may be reproduced, stored in any electronic system, or transmitted in any form or by any means, electronic, mechanical, photocopy, recording, or otherwise, without written permission from the author. Brief quotations may be used in literary reviews.

Printed by:
Pentecostal Publishing House
8855 Dunn Road
Hazelwood, MO 63042

CONTENTS

    Preface 7
    Dedication 9
1. The View from the Back of the Pulpit 11
2. Where Will You Go? What Will You Do? 15
3. The Firebird Stage 21
4. Does a Preacher Need a License? 25
5. The Minister's Self-Image 37
6. Of Saints and Reprobates 49
7. Respect 57
8. Shepherds or Sheep Transporters? 63
9. Surviving Church Storms 67
10. That Vision Thing 73
11. Walk with Me 85
12. Who Are These People? 91
13. Communication: Beyond the Basics 99
14. You Can't Just Change One Thing 107
15. Read Writers and Right Readers 115
16. The Power to Destroy or the
     Power to Redeem 119
17. Expensive Convictions 123
18. When Leaders Sin 129
19. Issues in Retirement for Pastors 145

PREFACE

I relish thumbing through a book about preachers and finding that the author nails it. Too many of us muddle around, up to our eyeballs in church work and knee-deep in people's problems, wondering what in the world we're doing. Is there is a better way? Do others struggle with the same challenges? Even if the writer doesn't have all the answers, I love it when at least he asks the same questions I am asking. My blood pressure dips enough to tell me I'm muddling in the normal range.

The title piece, "The View from the Back of the Pulpit," brings the normal range into focus for many pastors. It answers to the unfocused view of ministry held by many pew occupants who see nothing but the front of the pulpit. They see the ministry played out on a narrow screen. Preachers, however, need to know what other preachers say and think about ministry, their calling, and their fellowship. I hope that these chapters will yield some fresh insight to them, plus a measure of comfort and inspiration to boot.

Transparency in communication eludes too many of us in ministry. We have learned to be careful—some might say cowardly—because the same openness that produces trust also involves risk. Our lives are risky enough without playing in the traffic. Yet few significant things happen in life until we traffic in truth. Telling ourselves the truth requires courage, but it brings clarity to the mission. I hope I have cracked open the door to that truth a little more for my readers.

DEDICATION

I dedicate this volume to the wonderful ministers of the Ohio District of the United Pentecostal Church, International, whom I have been privileged to serve for many years. They have been an endless source of joy for me in ministry, in organizational matters, and in personal friendships. A finer group of consecrated men does not exist in Oneness Pentecostal circles. Together, we have shouted and danced, wept and prayed, counseled and conversed, agreed and disagreed, yet always loved and respected each other. They have allowed me to preside over their business, ordain them, install them, dedicate their buildings, preach their anniversaries, and write my editorials to them. And beyond the official and ministerial aspects, they have enriched me spiritually through their impact on my life. May all their visions become realities in their selfless work for God.

Chapter 1
The View from the Back of the Pulpit

Be not afraid of their faces (Jeremiah 1:8).

The worn spots that had been rubbed unevenly into each side of the pulpit by the old preacher's trembling hands came strangely into focus. I had been slowly scanning the sanctuary from the chair behind the pulpit, hoping for one last flicker of inspiration before speaking. Chandeliers, wooden pews, and other elements typical of the 1950s church decor had oscillated in and out of my peripheral vision. My eyes, narrowing now on the back of the sacred desk, saw that forty years of sermons, Bible studies, prayer meetings, announcements, invocations, and benedictions had turned the varnish gummy and slightly grimy. Had some persnickety types seen it from my perspective, they might have regarded it as evidence of neglect. Handymen may have made a mental note about a long overdue maintenance project. I saw something more. I saw a poignant testimony to a faithful servant of God, a student of the Word, a man with the call to preach and a burden for the

The View from the Back of the Pulpit

flock. Early on, he bounded up to his preaching post, bursting with energy and passion; much later, he struggled to climb the steps, futilely trying to hide the pain in his knees as he ascended. The thing that didn't wane over the years was his commitment to duty.

My eyes wandered to the back wall. The clock always let the old preacher know how fast his time was slipping away. Often, just after he had broken into a good sweat, the speeding minute hand poured cold water on the hottest of fires; the same hand drug with interminable slowness for the few teenagers and scattered youngsters held hostage in the pews. My dad always said he didn't mind if people looked at their watches. He just didn't like the people holding them to their ears to see if the pieces were still ticking. The clock is for the preacher. That's why it's on the back wall instead of the front.

> For every distraction registered in front of the pulpit, from the back of the pulpit God amplifies and magnifies the faces and voices that speak of spiritual hunger.

The view from the back of the pulpit can be daunting. The traffic. The latecomers. The early leavers. The bumps-on-logs. The live wires. The break-away toddlers. The weak-kidneyed multi-trippers, the restroom checker-outers. The door-slammers, note-passers, gum-chewers, picture-admirers, back-scratchers, nose-blowers, compact-viewers, nail-clipperers, window-gazers, light-bulb-counters, day-dreamers, baby-entertainers, homework-finishers, hair-combers, cat-nappers, face-makers, eye-rollers, child-

The View from the Back of the Pulpit

scolders, conversationalists, snorers, fidgeters, readers, doodlers, and the entire three-ring circus that a church service can become. While most just see the backs of heads and pews, the old preacher sees all the rest.

And that's not to mention the peeling paint, the smudges of little handprints on the wall, the burned-out bulbs, the wrinkled carpet, the water-stained ceiling tile, the stuck window, the door squeaking on the hinges, the disheveled literature rack, the shredded Kleenex under the front pew, and the wilted flowers from last Sunday's service. He wonders where the sound man is, why the guitarist is sitting in the congregation instead of in the orchestra section, and why the ushers are talking to each other instead of attending to a visitor's needs. He agonizes over the prospect of reaching all points on the spectrum: the newcomer, the couple with marriage problems, the discouraged saint, the fired-up new convert, and the antsy adolescent, all with the same sermon or Bible study. He knows that some want him to be funny; others want him to be somber. Still others want him to stick to his notes, and others yet want him to throw aside his notes and launch out into the spiritual deep. The dilemma's horns are not built for comfort.

But God giveth more grace. The preacher sees the faces. For every distraction registered in front of the pulpit, from the back of the pulpit God magnifies the faces and amplifies the voices of the spiritually hungry. The eyes welled with tears, the trembling lips, the intercessor's anguish, the hand waving in worship, the attentive listener, the revelatory moment of the spiritually enlightened, the prayer warrior, the impassioned heart, and the receptive spirit—these sights deliver a greater impact on the preacher than all the chaos

The View from the Back of the Pulpit

put together. God's amazing filter blocks out the distractions and equalizes the sensitivity of his servant to the spiritual needs that pervade a congregation. That's why he keeps on preaching through the chaos.

The old preacher has now moved. He no longer sees the church from the back of the pulpit. His body lies in state in front of the pulpit on his funeral day. But today he sees the church from yet another view—the one above the pulpit. He sees the church that God sees.

That he might present it to himself a glorious church, not having spot, or wrinkle, or any such thing; but that it should be holy and without blemish (Ephesians 5:27).

The preacher's lifelong challenge was to make his view match God's view. I think he succeeded.

Chapter 2
Where Will You Go?
What Will You Do?

Lord, we know not whither thou goest; and how can we know the way? (John 14:5).

Some time ago, a young minister asked me to pray for him to receive a definite direction from God for his ministry. Several successive moves had left him more confused about where he belonged and what he should be doing. Pressures other than the ministry compounded his problem —like finding a job with a decent wage, taking care of his family, and feeling like he was truly making a contribution. Lots of people had advice for him, some of it helpful, some of it free and worth every dime of it.

He is not alone. Letters and phone calls from ministers reach me regularly, asking if there are any pastorate openings or other opportunities in the district I serve. Some of them send me a resume. Nearly all of them express a desire for prayer that God will lead them into a productive ministry. The process can be brutal.

The View from the Back of the Pulpit

Breaking into the ministry seems like a distant and cloudy memory for most established ministers. Once they reach the point where they want to be, they often take for granted the open doors that led them there. Some of us were blessed with successful minister fathers or other relatives in pastoral leadership. In our organization, a man's name alone often creates an opening for him. Others have gotten a leg up by great men who mentored them, or were advantaged by prominent churches that lent them their influence. I don't for one minute think I am where I am without concessions made to me due to my background. (I will say: Someone may provide the opening, but afterward, a young minister had better produce or "put some corn in the crib," as the old-timers used to say, or he will not make it.)

But many young ministers struggle to find their niche. Without recognizable names or other intangible assets paving the way for them, they meet with closed doors, forbidden fields, sympathetic but unhelpful leaders, and discouraging circumstances. For them, finding success in the ministry seems like a formidable or even impossible task. What should they do? Should they evangelize? Should they start a home mission church from scratch? Should they take a small congregation and get a job to support themselves? Should they just help in a local church? Should they apply for the Associates In Missions program? These questions need answers, but first it is necessary to understand the two broad directions in which a minister can go.

Two main focal points exist on the ministerial horizon:

Where Will You Go? What Will You Do?

ministry and *place*. Either a minister is consumed with a burden for a particular location without claiming any extraordinary ministry, or he gravitates to a specific kind of ministry without reference to any place. In my observation, if a minister with a narrowly defined ministry stays in one place too long, he becomes restless. If, on the other hand, he senses a burden for a certain place, he never finds contentment anywhere else. In any event, a minister may not come to this understanding until he has been in the ministry a good while. Patience, therefore, stabilizes him until he arrives at his personal ministerial revelation and direction.

Further refining each focal point, a minister who feels most comfortable emphasizing a certain kind of ministry may be a gifted teacher, a flaming evangelist, a prophet, or a leader used to inspire, organize, or assist. But he may also possess a special desire to reach a certain kind of people, as an ethnic group, an urban population, a socioeconomic segment of the country, or a certain age level. A unique target will give definition to his ministry. When his type of ministry is needed or he has an opportunity to reach a certain group of people, he remains motivated and committed.

Ministers with a higher motivation to reach out to a particular place, however, have less concern for the *kind* of ministry they have than *where* they minister. We often hear preachers say that God called them to a certain city or even to a special section of a city. The testimonies of our pioneers lead us to conclude that God undoubtedly places a definitive burden upon certain men to open up states, provinces, and countries for the gospel. Spiritual trailblazers often labored in specific areas for years with only meager visible evidence of revival before finally seeing a breakthrough. Their burden for that place kept them going, even when they had opportunities to go elsewhere.

Variations exist within the two scenarios. The call to a place can be limited to a certain length of time, or a minister with a specialized ministry can develop other abilities later. The broad themes of ministry and place, however, offer a young minister a starting point to think seriously about what God wants him to do. He cannot accomplish this by anxiously looking to others for direction. He must come to terms with his personal call, whether it is to focus on his special ministry or to settle into a specific location. It may take a period of trial and error. The errors can hurt and cost money, time, and pride, but no anointed ministry can develop without going through the fire. Sometimes it seems as if a few get all the breaks, and wonderful situations just fall into their laps. Even in those cases, however, fire will inevitably test every minister's mettle. Whatever he must go through, his goal must be to mount his pulpit one day with the confidence that he is in the perfect will of God. Only then can he minister with conviction and resolve.

In considering the focal point of place, several factors enter into the decision. If it is home to the minister, he enjoys a familiarity with the region. He may have an existing job or he has an increased likelihood of finding one. He has a ready-made support group of family and friends, plus many acquaintances that represent a potential harvest. Also, a greater measure of acceptance opens to him because he knows the culture, the colloquialisms, and regional differences. These factors put him years ahead of another minister from the outside. But, for others, the *regions beyond* refrain sounded by the apostle Paul echoes loudly as God calls them to unfamiliar places. It could be in a radically different part of the country. It could be in a remote place halfway around the world. The true deciding factor cannot be a calculated check-off of pros and cons but is the passion that pumps through the heart of a God-called man. This passion propels him to "stick it out" in the place of his calling against all odds.

The minister with a specialized ministry deals with different concerns. Whether it is preaching, teaching, ministry to youth or children, or music ministry, he begins to excel in a certain field. Pastors begin to take note of him, and opportunities develop for him to exercise his gifts. He finds himself concentrating on his field and honing his craft. Other aspects of the ministry do not interest him nearly as much as the part that he loves. Although he sometimes feels frustrated because of the limited scope of his field, he has little heart for anything else. In the past, specialized ministries were not always accepted. Presently, however, the church continues to push back the parameters of recognized ministry and incorporate niche ministries into its overall spiritual program. The specialist who wants to deliver a real impact must believe wholeheartedly in his ministry. He must pour himself into his calling without reservation. If God has gifted him for a specific niche, the doors will open.

With these observations firmly in mind, the young minister can begin to address the questions posed earlier in this chapter. Does he feel that God has a definite locale in which he belongs? Does he feel that his ministry cannot be restricted to one place? The answer cannot be found according to his feelings alone, because feelings can be fickle and misleading. He must hear from God. This concept

The View from the Back of the Pulpit

seems to frighten many young ministers more than anything else. They have been so accustomed to getting their direction from leadership that they cannot easily make the transition to their own direct line to God. But the same God who called them into the ministry in the first place will also show them the *what* and *where* of their calling. If a man has confidence in his calling, he can have confidence in his direction. Moreover, as he patiently probes for direction, confirming evidences will emerge along the way.

It is true, of course, that many situations require the invitation of other ministers or the approval of the organization. A minister cannot simply declare he is going to assist someone or he is going to preach a revival in a specific church, without the consent of the person in charge. How to communicate that desire calls for proper protocol and measured responses. Even a call to a certain place means following proper procedure according to agreed-upon rules.

Waiting for the right door to open does not signal failure on the part of God or man. Waiting is part of the process. Impatience, haste, and a wanton disregard for rules eventually lead to self-destruction. The call of God cannot be used as a battering ram to force a desired result. A young minister who tries to force a door to open because he feels God has called him to a certain ministry not only hurts himself; he may destroy the door also. Remember, the will of God is good, perfect, and acceptable (Romans 12:1-2).

> *But they that wait upon the LORD shall renew their strength; they shall mount up with wings as eagles; they shall run, and not be weary; and they shall walk, and not faint* (Isaiah 40:31).

Chapter 3
The Firebird Stage

When I became a man, I put away childish things (I Corinthians 13:11).

At twenty-one, I couldn't preach my way out of a wet paper bag, but when I drove up to the pastor's house in my new, yellow, 1968 Pontiac Firebird with a black vinyl top, his kids sure thought I was a cool evangelist. It wasn't four-on-the-floor, but it had a console with black bucket seats, plus an 8-track tape player. Truth was, it never ran all that great, mainly because I had dealer-installed air conditioning. The space for the compressor and other parts was too cramped, causing the motor to keep overheating.

Anyway, just before I got married, I traded in my pride and joy for a revolting green, 1970 Pontiac Catalina. It was one of those no-nonsense, old-man types, a big, four-door sedan with a cavernous trunk for the typical evangelist's paraphernalia. We loaded an electric guitar, steel guitar, a padded Kustom amplifier, accordion, saxophone, sewing machine, suitcases, boxes of books, and a hundred pairs of shoes in that trunk with room to spare. The back seat served

The View from the Back of the Pulpit

as a great traveling closet with wall-to-wall hanging clothes. We never could have stuffed half of everything we needed in the little Firebird with a greased shoe spoon. When I pulled up to the house in my green tank, the kids groaned but the pastor smiled approvingly.

I realized that the image I projected determined the way I was received among the ministry. I had reached that stage in my life where practicality governed all decisions. The Firebird stage, as fun as it was, had started to become a liability to me. Yes, I remember the twinge of hurt I felt when I drove away in my Catalina and left that little beauty sitting in the dealer's lot. But I knew that it had to be done. Maturity slowly transforms one's viewpoint. I saw that my absorption with flare and image interfered with the greater calling to do a work for the kingdom of God. Later, I opted for the ultimate in old-fogy transportation: a full-sized van. I even traded several more times for newer vans. (But, let it be known, I never stooped to one of those boxy station wagons with simulated-wood side panels!)

For the sake of my ministry, I could not prolong the Firebird stage. More importantly than the needed roominess in the trunk, I wanted to focus seriously on things that brought more than admiration, oohs and aahs, and possibly envy. To me, a sports car diverted me from my real goals. Actually, I discovered a principle that was borne out in all areas of life. It changed the way I spent my money, picked my clothes, and used my time. It even made an impact on

The Firebird Stage

my associations with people. I realized that the image I projected determined the way I was received among the ministry. They assigned to me certain expectations and defined my character when they laid eyes on that Firebird. Some may think that's unfair, but human relationships develop in complicated ways. Had I thrown a tantrum over the fairness issue, I could have easily ruined myself with the very people to whom I was called to minister.

Did I just grow up? Probably. Today, however, people seem to have a harder time with this than ever before. Too many little kids grow up way too fast, and too many older people act disgustingly juvenile. The kids can't always help it because of their immaturity, but the adults are another story. Something is wrong when a grandmother decks out in bizarre, faddish outfits, as though she were a rebellious teenager. Something is equally wrong when a sixty-some-odd man comes roaring through town astride a Harley-Davidson, his braided gray hair flying from beneath a kerchief wrapped tightly around his head and every inch of bare skin decorated with tattoos and body piercings. Either people like this live in serious denial of their advancing age, or they reject the responsibilities dictated by their more mature roles in life. Whichever the case, they forfeit the important influence they could have on the upcoming generation. I believe the real problem revolves around unmitigated selfishness. Those forever stuck in the young and irresponsible stage care little for others who look to them for guidance and inspiration. They may have a right to express themselves in a free country, but that right does not obligate anyone else to accept them as role models.

A fine line often exists between mere youthfulness and

The View from the Back of the Pulpit

immaturity. We can be serious without being morbid. We can be conservative without being old-fashioned. We can be upbeat without being giddy. The serious servant of God needs to find that fine line and follow it. Whatever we do, people must see an absolute seriousness that defines our walk with God. Foolishness must not characterize a minister's behavior. The motivation for this refinement goes beyond the simple differences between right and wrong. It grows out of an insatiable desire to be like Jesus. When we get rid of the adolescent drags on our spirituality, we become free to move up and on.

Chapter 4
Does a Preacher Need a License?

Know them which labour among you (I Thessalonians 5:12).

Licensing its members represents the most critical function that a ministerial organization performs. Licensing screens applicants for membership eligibility, ensures uniformity in doctrine, and enforces behavioral guidelines for individual members. The importance of this function cannot be overstated. The singular authority of the United Pentecostal Church, International, to grant or withhold a license ultimately governs its very nature and purpose. Why? Because, as it has been said, "As go the people, so goes the church." And as go the ministers, so goes an organization. All policies, provisions, rules, regulations, programs, missions, and visions proceed directly out of the hearts of the constituents.

Although cynics may think that organization was hatched in the minds of power-hungry men, it actually evolved out of conditions that followed the early stages of

The View from the Back of the Pulpit

the twentieth-century revival. The times were so chaotic that they threatened to derail this spiritual upsurge. Strange doctrines and heretical ideologues took advantage of the movement's unregulated landscape and caused untold damage to many sincere congregations. Charlatans and unscrupulous characters, like the snake-oil salesmen of our country's history, infiltrated the loosely organized Pentecostal movement. The Scripture warns us to "know them which labour among you," but in those early days, spiritual imposters with a whoop and a holler, a little shaking of the head, and a few wild stories ravaged gullible believers, stole churches, and lined their pockets with misappropriated funds. It soon became evident that all would be lost unless the ministry found a way to regulate itself.

Recently, I initiated a discussion with several groups of ministers about why many young men aspiring to the ministry decline to apply for a minister's license. Judging from their responses, we need a renewed education in some basic organizational concepts. The major points they made are:

- A license won't make me a better preacher.
- I love the Apostolic message, but I have reservations about the organization.
- I disagree with some of the positions and doctrines of the UPCI.
- A license would just qualify me for an office, and I'm not interested in one.
- All that business and voting is boring.
- I can still preach anywhere that a licensed minister can.

Does a Preacher Need a License?

- I can preach better without a license than a lot of ministers can with a license.
- No one ever asks if I have a license anyway.
- I want to be free to preach in churches that would be off-limits if I had a license.
- Older ministerial friends and relatives have discouraged me from applying.
- The board intimidates me.
- I follow the dictates of my conscience, not the rulings of a board.
- I will someday, but not now.
- I can't afford to pay the dues.

In answering these objections, I am not coming from the standpoint of an organizational official. I held these views before I ever received my local license many years ago. Rather, I consider getting a ministerial license the only honorable thing to do, especially if a minister reaps the benefits of the organization. The tremendous advantage of belonging to an organization far outweighs any requirements asked of its members.

Let's now look at each of these reasons given for failing to join.

Objection #1: *A license won't make me a better preacher.* No, a piece of paper in your pocket or a certificate hanging on your wall will not make you a better preacher. A fishing license won't guarantee that you will catch fish either, nor will a marriage license make a man a better husband. A ministerial license does demonstrate that you have the approval of seasoned men of God who, after examining your qualifications, character, references, and understanding of the Bible, deem you worthy of belonging to a fellowship of like-minded ministers. Credentials will not replace continued study, prayer, and dedication to the ministry, but they do offer a form of protection to UPCI congregations as well as enhance a minister's standing with his peers.

Objection #2: *I love the Apostolic message, but I have reservations about the organization.* The answer to this objection is one of those principles that can be difficult to express on paper, but experience and observation through the years validate it. The purity and strength of the Apostolic message today have been vastly stabilized by a solid organization. No one claims that the UPCI or any other Oneness organization is perfect, but I would hate to see what would have happened to the Apostolic message without an organization(s) of ministers who remained accountable to each other as well as to God for the orthodoxy of their preaching and teaching. Reservations about organization should not mean rejection of organization.

Objection #3: *I disagree with some of the positions and doctrines of the UPCI.* Since those who hold this view continue to preach in UPCI churches, it seems to me that the disingenuousness of this argument ought to be apparent on its face. After all, why would anyone want to preach in churches—with or without a license—whose doctrines varied greatly from his own beliefs? Why would a preacher even fellowship with such people? For a paycheck? For pride? For career-enhancing opportunities? All the UPCI has ever asked is that its ministerial fellowship would come together in unity on certain fundamental doctrines and pursue harmony in everything else. This is probably true for every organization in existence on the planet, whether religious or secular.

Objection #4: *A license would just qualify me for an office, and I'm not interested in one.* I suspect that a layer of arrogance is lodged somewhere in this excuse offering. The UPCI is not comprised of office-holders. Moreover, unlicensed preachers who believe this must not think much of those who do hold license. Those persons elected or appointed to an office soon find that much work and responsibility go with the position. I have the utmost respect and appreciation for those who are willing to serve in any capacity for the good of the organization.

Objection #5: *All that conference business is boring.* True, but lots of us find important things—like paying taxes, voting, buying insurance, visiting certain relatives, drawing up legal documents, and standing in line for any reason—boring. That business may be boring, but it is far better than the chaos and conflict that would surely ensue without it. Grave decisions that shape ministries, affect churches, and govern lives find their way out of the mundane resolutions, reports, and yeas and nays of business meetings.

Objection #6: *I can still preach anywhere that a licensed minister can.* Then why don't preachers who say this advertise—or even celebrate—the fact that they are unlicensed? The truth is that they would rather not have anybody know. They want to blend in with the others without calling attention to their status.

Objection #7: *I can preach better without a license than a lot of ministers can with a license.* The converse is also true: many licensed preachers can preach better than unlicensed ones. What's the point, anyway? Neither possession of a license nor the lack of one creates a preacher. Licensing addresses much more than preaching ability. It is a statement about a minister's character, integrity, and doctrine. You might declare that you are a good person, but it means so much more when your brethren say it about you. Plenty of great communicators who dodge all accountability travel the preaching circuits and get lots of chances to ply their trade. So do nightclub performers, business club speakers, and politicians. The ministry holds itself to a much higher standard than platform performance.

Objection #8: *No one ever asks if I have a license anyway.* Most pastors already know if the preachers they ask to preach in their churches hold a license. If they don't know and don't ask, it's not necessarily because they don't care. Most of the time, they just assume that a preacher either has a license or seeks one. Nevertheless, it is a good practice for pastors to ask point-blank if a preacher has a license and the name of the group with which he is affiliated. Otherwise, he grants someone access to his pulpit whose doctrine, beliefs, and personal life may deviate widely from his own or may be extremely dangerous to the spiritual health of his congregation. Pastors who expose their people to fly-by-night pulpiteers are asking for headache and heartache. I envision that, in the future, UPCI pastors may be more inclined to ask about a license.

Objection #9: *I want freedom to preach in churches that are off-limits to licensed preachers.* In my experience, the only churches that have been declared off-limits are those that have a notorious reputation for lack of scruples. If a pastor of one of these churches has a moral blight on his ministry, if he has compromised his doctrine, or if he has built his congregation through sheep-stealing and other unprincipled tactics, why would a good man want to preach there anyway? Moreover, relatively few preachers have lost their license over preaching in questionable churches, although some may have been reprimanded from time to time. In my experience, the UPCI has been fair and reasonable in such cases.

Objection #10: *Older ministerial friends and relatives have discouraged me from applying.* As hard as this is to believe, I know that ministers who have been deeply hurt in the past by certain troubles with the organization may have talked young ministers out of a license. When they use their influence this way, they probably do not have the welfare of the prospective applicant in mind. More than likely, their anger and bitterness have never been resolved. Stopping someone else from joining the organization, even though they themselves may still belong, becomes a small form of revenge for them. Even sadder, the situations that caused their original hurt have probably long since disappeared. Yet ministers with past wounds continue to harbor ill will and negative feelings against the organization. When talking with them, keep in mind that their hurt skews their opinion.

Objection #11: *The board intimidates me.* Today's district boards are not nearly as intimidating as they were in past years. In my first experience before a board, the superintendent pulled his chair next to me, leaned into my face, and, in a loud voice, told me to explain John 17:5, "And now, O Father, glorify thou me with thine own self with the glory which I had with thee before the world was." I nearly passed out. I don't remember what I said, and it probably wasn't worth remembering anyway. These days, most applicants are not pistol-whipped. They are given the royal treatment and they are affirmed and encouraged. Still, it may not be a bad idea for some intimidation to take place. I would rather call it awe and respect. No district board should wave applicants through without careful examination, but neither should a board present a real obstacle to licensing a qualified preacher.

Objection #12: *I follow the dictates of my conscience, not the rulings of a board.* Any Apostolic minister who agrees with the fundamental doctrine of the organization should not have major disagreements with any district board. If he does, he needs to know that no board has more power than that given to it by the UPCI manual. If any minister objects to a board ruling, the UPCI provides for a Minister's Appeal Council to adjudicate grievances independently from the district. Perhaps the larger issue that someone with this problem needs to address is one of accountability or inability to submit to authority.

Objection #13: *I will someday, but not now.* This objection may be based more on circumstantial details than principle. A major move like joining the UPCI may be complicated for some ministers and can only be done at the expedient time. As far as principle is concerned, if it will be right in the future, why is it not right at the present? The need to belong and the benefits of belonging will not change. I encourage anyone who truly believes that getting a license is the right thing to do should do the right thing now.

Does a Preacher Need a License?

Objection #14: *I can't afford to pay the dues.* Our willingness to pay for anything is usually a function of its necessity. All of us find a way to afford goods and services that we can't live without. As expensive as membership in a ministerial organization may be, its loss or impaired ability to operate would be far more costly to us. Also, anyone who reaps the benefits of the organization has a moral and ethical obligation to support it.

Now that we have looked at some objections to licensing, let's consider the many positive benefits of becoming a member of an organization.

Benefit #1: *Official fellowship.* When a minister becomes licensed with the UPCI, he receives a certificate recognized by his peers, whether it be local, general, or ordination. Not only does this certification have significant personal meaning, it also has a legal effect on his status insofar as governmental agencies are concerned.

Benefit #2: *Representation on a national and international level.* Often, the UPCI speaks for the entire ministerial body to the nation. Our General Superintendent has written letters to the President of the United States from time to time on social, moral, and legal matters that pertain to the church. Official membership also incurs benefits to individual ministers such as the right to visit or administer baptism to incarcerated persons.

Benefit #3: *Right to have a voice and vote.* Every minister in the UPCI may influence the decisions made at the sectional, district, or national level. He may speak out in an official meeting of ministers, communicate with his elected officials, write his views and publish them himself, or send them to a district or general publication. Moreover, full-time ministers can vote for or against candidates or issues. Without a license, a minister has no such rights.

Benefit #4: *Practical, informal fellowship.* One of the great joys of belonging to the UPCI continues to be the rich and edifying fellowship among the ministering brethren. Licensed ministers have a compelling reason to converse with their colleagues about organizational matters, plans and developments on a national or international scale, and all the people who perform various tasks in the organization. They share in the give-and-take of social dynamics that take place among those who occupy common ground.

Benefit #5: *Other rights, privileges, and benefits.* Since the UPCI is a recognized, ordaining body, each minister has a legitimate basis for ordination. The organization represents him and protects him. He can appeal to the judicial procedure if he is ever accused of misconduct. In case he encounters problems in his local church, he can automatically appeal to a presbyter or district superintendent to stand with him. He also maintains insurance or other benefits provided by the organization. Licensed ministers draw much strength from the backing of an organization.

Benefit #6: *Opportunity for ministerial functions.* Licensed ministers are eligible to participate in functions of the UPCI at any level. If appointed or elected, they can belong to committees or boards, not as mere observers but as participants in crafting policy and making decisions.

Benefit #7: *Access to special ministries in the UPCI.* Children and youth of churches pastored by licensed ministers may attend UPCI functions such as camps, retreats, and conferences with their pastors' signatures on their registration forms. They can come by right, not mere courtesy.

Does a Preacher Need a License?

Benefit #8: *Access to UPCI Bible colleges.* As in the case of youth and children's camps, Bible college applicants need the signature of a UPCI pastor. If a student's pastor is not a member of the UPCI, he or she is at a clear disadvantage from applicants from UPCI churches.

Benefit #9: *Hosting privileges.* Hosting a district conference, a rally, or some other special meeting proves to be a tremendous blessing and privilege to a church congregation. These meetings expose local community and church members to the ministry of highly respected and renowned men of God, and they see the wide influence and stature of the organization. Local pastors gain stature and strength from their involvement in the UPCI.

Benefit #10: *Input into divisional or departmental ministry.* God has blessed many ministers with a wonderful creative ability and a vision that extends far beyond their local church. The UPCI affords a venue for expressing and utilizing these talents at every level. Whether in administration, Christian education, youth work, planting churches, foreign missions service, or some other field, a UPCI minister may find fulfillment in organizational work.

Benefit #11: *Freedom to engage UPCI ministers to preach.* UPCI pastors enjoy an unrestricted right to ask anyone who is licensed with the organization to come to speak in their pulpit without requesting clearance. Our protocol stipulates for UPCI pastors to get special permission before engaging any non-affiliated ministers to preach. This provision helps to protect the integrity of the fellowship.

Would it be better to remain unlicensed? Members of the United Pentecostal Church, International, are well aware of other Oneness Pentecostal ministers who choose not to affiliate. While some belong to other organizations, many others prefer to stay independent. The tests of time, however, confirm the needs and benefits of organization. I contend that licensing expands a minister's effectiveness and ministerial potential far beyond the level he could otherwise reach. But not only does a preacher need a license for his personal benefit; the ministerial body as a whole needs the strength of the organization to be effective. In our diverse and mobile society, organization ensures uniformity on major tenets of faith. When the UPCI first formed, ministers commonly understood this. Today, many third- and fourth-generation Apostolics have not had to think about it very much because the organization just *is*. They lack exposure to the chaos, the brutal power struggles, and the general frustration that beset early twentieth-century Apostolics. Organization grew out of necessity.

Organization among ministers cannot exist without responsible fellowship. This means that what I do or fail to do affects you; what you do or fail to do affects me. We need to be accountable, submissive, and respectful to each other. Sometimes this goes against the grain, but we cannot expect the blessings of fellowship if we are unwilling to shoulder the difficulties. When I received my ministerial license, I affirmed that my beliefs and convictions may not be *perfectly* but are *best* represented by the UPCI Articles of Faith. I am not saying that I am 100 percent in favor of every line, jot, and tittle of the UPCI Manual. I have a conviction that I ought to submit to provisions that I may not personally like. That is responsible fellowship. It is not always easy, but it is always best.

Chapter 5
The Minister's Self-Image

For if a man think himself to be something . . . (Galatians 6:3).

Few callings outside the ministry demand such a total blend of professional qualifications with personal character. Anyone who goes forward with a ministerial career must understand that one's true personality and character are inextricably woven into the calling.

Before any aspirant takes the first step to turning a dream into a reality, he or she should be prepared to answer these questions: "Who am I? Do I really know myself? Why am I the way I am?" Self-analysis may be difficult, but every prospective minister has to know basic facts about his or her true self and be able to interpret those facts as objectively as possible. Superficial answers to questions such as name, gender, race, height, weight, family background, and other details that identify us will not suffice here. The quest must go deeper than the obvious.

To bring the question of personal identity into sharper focus, let us look at other traits. In socioeconomic terms, do you consider yourself upper, middle, or lower class? Do you come from a high-, moderate-, or low-income family? Do you possess skills or talents that are recognized by others, or are you simply an average person? Are you athletic? Are you attractive or plain? What is your IQ? What is the extent of your education?

What is your range of interests? Are you a reader? Do you like to talk to people? Do you prefer a dynamic, changing environment or are you more comfortable in dealing with solid and stable situations? Are you traditional and predictable or can you be creative and wild? When you were growing up, were you exposed to a variety of cultural or geographical settings? Are you a homebody or do you have a penchant for travel? The answers to these questions help to reveal your true identity.

Even further, can you identify your basic personality? Is your health good? Have you had serious physical problems in the past? Were your parents permissive or strict disciplinarians? Have you been a failure or a success in your life's endeavors? Have you suffered from discrimination or prejudice? Have you been touched by death, divorce, or personal tragedy? Are you a victim of physical, sexual, psychological, or emotional abuse? These questions may seem improper and too personal. You may even feel that they are irrelevant to the anointing and call of God on your life. Perhaps you look at negative experiences in your life as mere obstacles to be overcome, or you consider your positive attributes as enhancing your ministry. Whatever your reaction to this self-examination may be, it is vital for you to understand the things that define you as a person. They represent your ground zero. Your truthful answers

The Minister's Self-Image

will give you a frank, honest, and real beginning to your ministry.

Investigating one's personal past is difficult because truth often hurts. Addressing truths that have been long buried and denied may be particularly excruciating. You will undoubtedly dredge up defining moments when you felt rejection, ridicule, loss, and embarrassment. Do it anyway. Calvin Miller, in *The Empowered Leader*, says, "Self-analysis is hard work! It is tiring work! It is endless work!" But the anticipated outcome has less to do with psychological or emotional well-being than with a deep understanding of how you affect the people you lead. Your influence, your effectiveness, and your relationships—all your real-life circumstances—grow inexorably out of your identity.

In the Bible, those who played significant roles emerged from diverse backgrounds. Their usefulness as God's servants was profoundly affected by their differing experiences. Moses, for example, came of age in Pharaoh's courts. This directly influenced his call to return to Egypt to lead the Israelites out of slavery. His experiences as an infant who escaped a massacre, as a fugitive from the law, and as a shepherd for forty years in the desert tempered his leadership. Moses also had a very noticeable speech impediment. "And Moses said unto the LORD, O my Lord, I am not eloquent, neither heretofore, nor since thou hast spoken unto thy servant: but I am slow of speech, and of a slow tongue" (Exodus 4:10). One could argue that this weakness significantly shaped Moses' personality and demeanor.

Examples of these phenomena exist throughout the Bible. Leaders like Saul, David, Daniel, Isaiah, Paul, and Peter bore unmistakable influences of their experiences and

The View from the Back of the Pulpit

culture upon their leadership. In fact, one cannot possibly understand these men and the decisions they made without carefully examining their roots. Judging from some individuals—King David and the apostle Paul, for instance—it is clear that God chose special people for certain roles because of their unique individual traits. This fact is strongly borne out in Paul's letter to the Philippians.

> *Though I might also have confidence in the flesh. If any other man thinketh that he hath whereof he might trust in the flesh, I more: Circumcised the eighth day, of the stock of Israel, of the tribe of Benjamin, an Hebrew of the Hebrews; as touching the law, a Pharisee; concerning zeal, persecuting the church; touching the righteousness which is in the law, blameless. But what things were gain to me, those I counted loss for Christ. Yea doubtless, and I count all things but loss for the excellency of the knowledge of Christ Jesus my Lord: for whom I have suffered the loss of all things, and do count them but dung, that I may win Christ* (Philippians 3:4-8).

While Paul renounced any spiritual value of these events and earmarks of his upbringing, he still referred to them, for they formed the backdrop to his devotion to Christ and to his ministry. Had they been insignificant details of his past, referencing them would have had little value. The force of Paul's apostleship, while it was definitely a product of his encounter with God on the road to Damascus, still consisted largely of his former identity with the Judaistic hierarchy and of his personality traits of zeal and passion.

The Minister's Self-Image

Over one hundred years ago, sociologist Edwin H. Sutherland proposed a theory about the origins of delinquency and crime. His theory, differential association, posited that youth learn criminal behavior through social interaction with others. As they associate with intimate, personal groups, they adapt to the behavior and core beliefs of those groups.

Although Sutherland focused specifically on criminals, scholars have applied his idea to other venues. The result is that differential association has been validated in many other applications. Actually, the theory is an enlargement on the old maxim that "birds of a feather flock together." First Corinthians 15:33 says, "Be not deceived: evil communications corrupt good manners." The principle Sutherland articulated explains the process by which all of us develop our identities, and can define the end result of the process with a fair amount of accuracy.

Today, every minister represents a composite of background experiences, cultural identities, mind-sets, dysfunctions, biases, and values. Like a color chart with thousands of shades, these traits exist in varying degrees, forms, and strengths. If a minister is unmindful of this—and many times even with intimate self-knowledge—his strongest thrust will be exerted toward those ideals and values that are closest to the heart.

Consider for a moment how different people from differing backgrounds and experiences would approach their ministries: A former Navy SEAL, a college professor, a star athlete, a former Marine sergeant, a factory worker, a successful farmer, a union official, a former gang leader, a person delivered from alcohol, a former drug addict, a computer expert, a musician, the founder of a business, a truck driver, a contractor, a pastor's daughter or son. In my observation of ministers with these or similar backgrounds, the style and tone of their ministries have been largely predictable along the lines of their past training. The SEAL values intensity and focus; the college professor emphasizes intellectual pursuits; the athlete brings supreme confidence to the pulpit; the Marine expects military-like responses from his congregation, and so on.

What impact would personal characteristics such as obesity, an amputated limb, a strikingly handsome appearance, superior intelligence, or a thick accent have on an individual's ministry? Is one's ministry affected if he or she is unmarried? Does it matter if the minister is married and has several children? What if the minister lost a child to disease or an accident? We could go on creating endless scenarios. Regardless of the circumstances, a high probability exists that each factor will create a unique and discernable difference in a person's ministry. Ministers will demonstrate a bias toward those deeply held personal traits with which they identify the strongest. While the spiritual side of the ministerial equation remains constant from person to person, this human side differs dramatically. This means that the minister's effectiveness will never be solely a function of God's power and faithfulness. It will also reflect the minister's response to his or her own humanity.

> Your personal identity will profoundly influence your ministerial style, your goals, your decisions and proclaimed values.

The Minister's Self-Image

Let's put this as plainly as possible: Your personal identity will profoundly influence your ministerial style, your goals, your decisions and proclaimed values. Not only will this principle be borne out in your ministry, it cannot be any other way. You cannot be someone you are not, nor can you deny who you are. In a sense, you are pre-programmed to operate in a certain mode.

Several observations need to be made about the way you see yourself and how it may affect your ministry.

Know your personal strengths and weaknesses. This step involves two things: awareness and admission. First, you must be aware of the kinds of strengths and weaknesses you possess, and second, you must admit that they make a difference in your leadership and ministry. For example, a minister raised in an abusive environment will show telltale signs of those painful experiences—whether in preaching, teaching, counseling, goal-setting, or decision-making. Any attempt to deny this bias will lead to false constructs for leadership and bring about noticeable consequences. This minister may develop harshness in tone or become sarcastic, demanding, negative, or mistrustful. Unless the connection can be made between ministry and background, the minister may never fully understand the forces that drive him or her.

In *The Empowered Leader*, Calvin Miller refers to David's encounter with Goliath to illustrate this point.

> *David, in I Samuel 17:26, was a person in touch with both his limitations and the unlimited power of God. He turned outward to consider the crisis, not thinking of all his personal weaknesses. No paralysis*

The View from the Back of the Pulpit

intimidated David! What was to be done? David was not sure: wringing his hands would not help.

Then come questions from a foe that David must first process and then reply to: "Who is this uncircumcised Philistine that he should defy the armies of the living God?" (I Samuel 17:26, NIV). David must first answer Goliath's question, not so Goliath will know who David is, but so that David himself will know who David is. Without knowing who he is, David cannot assess his strengths and weaknesses and be reminded of his need to depend on God.

Understand why you are passionate about certain things. When you listen to numerous preachers over a long period of time, you can discern a good sermon from a great one. Good sermons may be homiletically correct and scripturally sound, but they may not inspire their audiences. In contrast, great messages may lack some qualities of good sermon crafting, but they flow out of a passionate heart and evoke great responses. Most preachers get excited over certain topics. Some call them "candy sticks" or "hot buttons." These topics, whatever they may be, usually fire them up. As we reflect on this trait, the operative question to ask is why. The obvious answer is that we become emotional over subjects that touch a nerve, subjects that connect us to some deeply moving experience or feeling in our past. Do you know what stirs your passions? If you don't know, find out. When you find out, ask why.

Passion finds expression in avenues of ministry besides the pulpit. Passion influences vision casting, counseling sessions, business procedures and decisions, physical plant

The Minister's Self-Image

management, leadership training, interpersonal relationships, and many other areas of ministerial functions. You will revert over and over to habits, opinions, and positions that have the greatest significance in your life. Again, the point is not necessarily to interpret or even change your feelings (unless they are wrong), but to understand the forces and events that drive you.

What responses do you elicit from the people God has called you to serve? Do they support you? Resist you? Ignore you? Listen to you? The value of self-inquiry lies in this analysis. If you find success and blessing in your ministry, don't just wave it off. You need to know why. Similarly, when you go through inevitable times of difficulty, don't begin to copy someone else's ministry. Many times, successful ministers get off message as they experiment with things that don't work for them. People will tend to respond positively to your strengths but negatively to your weaknesses.

On the other hand, if your words or actions cause people to scratch their heads and wonder what's going on or if you find yourself constantly antagonizing and frustrating the saints, you may think something is wrong with them. Some ministers address this situation by increasing their decibel level, displaying anger, or lacing their sermons with sarcasm and thinly-veiled references to church members. Others quote Scripture excessively that reinforces their position but avoid passages that mitigate against them. These mechanisms do not offer effective solutions. Greater understanding does. When you seek to understand yourself, you wind up understanding others as well.

How do you begin this journey of self-examination? Try

The View from the Back of the Pulpit

using sentences like, "The reason I say _____ is because I heard my father say _____ so often." Or "I wonder if I always do _____ because I remember what happened when I was _____." Also, listen carefully to criticism you may receive from certain people outspoken enough to give it to you. Before assigning a malicious motive to their comments, ask yourself if there is an element of truth to what they say. You will never understand if you always jump on the defensive. This may be a divinely ordained opportunity to learn. Run the criticism by a mentor or a friend so he can coach you for a moment. If you want to be coached effectively, accept and heed criticism.

In summary, these are the important steps you must take in understanding who you are and why you do what you do.

- Know your background.
- Do not allow your strengths to replace the power of God in your ministry.
- Do not allow your weaknesses to stop you from succeeding in the ministry.
- Do not frustrate yourself by comparing your ministry with that of others.
- Compensate for the areas in which you are lacking.

Oswald Sanders in his classic work, *Spiritual Leadership*, included this insightful quotation: "A great statesman made a speech that turned the tide in national affairs. 'May I ask how long it took you to prepare that speech?' asked an admirer. 'All my life has been a preparation for what I said today,' was the reply."

As you stand at the threshold of a call into the ministry,

The Minister's Self-Image

your focus may center on the deep, compelling desire you have to work for God. You feel a strange combination of excitement and anxiety, of anticipation and dread, and of faith in God's empowerment and fear of your own inadequacies. The thrust of your desire may be so strong, however, that you may run past some very significant stops along the way. You must never forget that the divine impetus that drives you can only work through the human faculties that you possess. You are the filter through which God ministers to the people in your care.

Chapter 6
Of Saints and Reprobates

And love unto all the saints . . . (Ephesians 1:15).
. . . *men of corrupt minds, reprobate concerning the faith* (II Timothy 3:8).

A mystifying maze of people problems confronts ministers on a daily basis. Why is it that among any given group, some people emerge as genuine gifts of God to the ministry, while others, in the same group, delight in causing pastoral breakdowns? How does the identical environment produce people at opposite ends of the spectrum? Do we unwittingly create these personalities or do we simply inherit them? And regardless of how they end up in our sheepfold, do we comprehend them, cope with them, or just categorize them? Every leader in the kingdom of God tries to make some sense of it all.

Broadly speaking, people fall into two categories: saints and reprobates. A saint typifies the ideal characteristics of virtue, honor, and holiness. The term "reprobate," however, describes people who have no spiritual value. They are the dross or the castaways of Scripture who fail every test of discipleship. We can further divide these groups into subgroups or classes. I'll start with the reprobate category first, so we can get the negative nastiness behind us.

The Reprobates

The Ignorant. The term "reprobate" may be too severe for this person, but everybody starts somewhere. The Bible regards this person as simple, unlearned, and untaught. Peter called them "babes." "As newborn babes, desire the sincere milk of the word, that ye may grow thereby" (I Peter 2:2). The ignorant person simply has little or no knowledge of true right and wrong. He most likely grew up in a moral vacuum without the benefit of training in conscience or rudimentary Bible knowledge. He needs rigorous teaching to fill in his knowledge gaps. Most of the immoral deeds he does stem from a profound ignorance of truth. I hold high hopes for this person. If he responds positively to solid teaching, he may redefine his life and become an asset to the kingdom.

The Problem. Many individuals have an adequate knowledge of good and evil and can probably quote numerous verses of Scripture, but they willfully disobey the clear mandates of the Word of God and even rebel against their spiritual authority. Sometimes they simply struggle with a weak character or they can be easily influenced by the wrong people. Others require high maintenance in order to do right, and when they don't get it, they bog down in their own personal quagmire. These types can drive a pastor to distraction, not so much by dissension but by disobedience. Frequent visits to the office never seem to change their bad habits. Usually, they don't cause problems; they *are* problems. As a pastor, I try to lift them as high as I can, but if they refuse to grow, I do not allow them to interfere with my ministerial duties to the entire church.

The Rebel. This person creates serious difficulties for all pastors and churches. Like the problem person, he too has acquired a measure of skill in scriptural use and also resists any pastoral authority over him. His treachery, however, lies in his desire to wield influence over other people. He is not content simply to go his own contrary way. He stirs up other people and poisons them with his rebellion as well. He is especially hard to deal with because of his ability to enlist others to his cause, in particular, the ignorant and problem people as previously defined. Whenever the pastor attempts to discipline him, a church-wide crisis erupts. He compounds every problem, regardless of how small it may be, through lies, distortions, and gossip. He is adept at deflecting criticism and turning it into an unfair attack on himself or his family. Sometimes, he even uses it as "proof" of pastoral abuse. You will always find this kind of person at the bottom of every church split. The Rebel often hangs himself because he is driven by wrong motives, but before that happens he can inflict much damage to a church. Deal with him prayerfully, carefully, and with a sure footing in the Word of God.

The Revolutionary. This person rises up as an icon of rebellion to an entire group or even to a generation. He combines superior intelligence and abilities with a familiarity of the Bible to reach beyond a local church as he targets an entire city or district. The Revolutionary sees himself as an intellectual hero to disenchanted, disgruntled people everywhere and feeds their resistance with books, tapes, and pamphlets designed to sever their connections to pastors. With the advent of the Internet era, he sends mass emails or even manages a Web site dedicated to church doctrine or leadership. He not only wants to destroy old alliances, but he also tries to forge new relationships, perhaps even new organizations. Alexander, Hymenaeus, and Philetus (I Timothy 1:20; II Timothy 2:17) represent these villains. Because their radical doctrines and insidious methods created such a menace to the whole church, the apostle Paul publicly denounced them.

In my ministerial career and my time as an official, I have been forced to deal with all of the above. Other than the foregoing paragraphs, I have no pearls of wisdom to offer so a leader can succeed every time. I thank God, however, that the saints always outnumber the reprobates! For every troublemaker, ten saints step forward to provide support and stability in the midst of it all. Here are the subdivisions of saints.

> For every troublemaker, ten saints step forward to provide support and stability in the midst of it all.

The Saints

The Novice. Having recently emerged from the ranks of sin, this person walks around starry-eyed and awed by the presence of God. He is curious about everything and he constantly asks questions about routine church life that everyone else takes for granted. Sometimes he goes to excess, sometimes he says and does things that break the rules, but he responds quickly to correction. Though he's not there yet, we should never forget that the Novice is a saint in the making. Teach him and train him, but also challenge him to stretch into maturity. You may need to assign him to a mentor, but don't neglect him. He may be loaded with far more potential than you imagine.

The Disciple. This person has matured into a faithful saint of God. He comes to service regularly, pays tithes and offerings, worships, adheres to holiness teaching, and manifests a positive attitude about life in general. He enjoys preaching and teaching and grasps the fundamentals of Apostolic doctrine. He helps on workdays, accepts responsibilities such as ushering, singing in the choir, or driving the church van, and has few occasions to seek pastoral counsel. Once in a while, if he loses a job or if he suffers a death in the family, the ebb and flow of life can get him down. He always rebounds, however, and you will see him back in his usual place, worshiping, smiling, and shaking hands. The Disciple forms the backbone of the church. He may not show charisma or remarkable personal qualities, but make sure you love him, appreciate him, and treat him right. With only a modicum of attention, he will always be there for you.

The Leader. This person has progressed through the novice and discipleship stage and continues to grow. He possesses a true affection for spiritual ideals, and some would even call it a burden for the growth and stability of the church. The most striking feature of this person, however, is his ability to influence others to be better and do more. Assign him a task, and soon an organized effort

The View from the Back of the Pulpit

develops that surpasses the initial objective. Talk to him about some of your wishes and dreams, and they begin to take on real substance through his efforts. Left alone, he finds positive uses of his time and energy. He spots weak people and strengthens them. He inspires others through his heartening and uplifting attitude. When you need someone to shoulder some responsibility, he immediately comes to mind. Every church needs a few people like the Leader. Without him, the pastor cannot function for long. With just one or two of these types, the load not only gets lighter, the church can also take quantum leaps forward. The one precaution with this person is not to overload him without commensurate reward. Also, be willing to share the ministry with its attendant credit and glory.

The Minister. As colleges make distinctions between bachelors, masters, and doctoral degrees, we must also recognize a pronounced difference between the church leader and the person who is destined for a much higher level. He experiences a calling from God on his life that surpasses a feeling of loyalty to a church or pastor. He genuinely understands that his entire life has been reformulated to revolve around a divine mission. He may be a visionary and see the big picture. He may even be able to understand the larger relationships between God, churches, organizations, and the world itself. The Minister integrates the virtues of the new convert, discipleship, and leadership into the passionate pursuit of a universal purpose. A person of obviously superior capabilities, his innate talents remain subjected to the will of God. This person may become a pastor or an evangelist, but perhaps he will be an apostle, a spiritual father, or a gospel pioneer. He aspires not to his own greatness but to the triumph of the church. Should the pathway of the Minister begin under your leadership, pray that God helps you to recognize what's happening and then watch it happen. The rise of the true minister becomes inexorable early on, and he soon starts feeding from a source that may well be beyond your own level. You could possibly be witnessing a contributing force in shaping history.

As church leaders, God will not put on us any more than we can bear. He will give us the grace to deal with the reprobates and the wisdom to guide the saints. The Bible teaches us that the wheat and the tares must at times grow together. Thus, we cannot always use aggressive measures to get the desired results. The best we can do is to understand the behavior patterns of the people in our charge and design our actions accordingly.

Chapter 7
Respect

Be kindly affectioned one to another with brotherly love; in honour preferring one another (Romans 12:10).

I'll never forget it. He called me into the office during a local church conference. A dozen or so preachers were standing around, shooting the breeze. As a young minister, unlicensed at the time, I was anxious to make a good impression. After all, he was widely known and respected. I had preached for him one Sunday earlier that summer.

"What's the matter, son?" he asked loudly enough for everyone in the room to hear. "Don't you have any money?"

"What do you mean?" I asked.

"I said, 'Don't you have any money?' *Are you deaf or an idiot?*"

Embarrassed, I said something like, "Y–y–yes. . . . Why?"

He reached into his pocket, pulled out a five-dollar bill, and stuck it out to me. "Because I thought if you had enough money, you would have gotten yourself a haircut before you came to conference!" With that, he glanced around the room, and his shoulders started to shake with laughter. His buddies howled and slapped one another on the back.

My face turned red and I left that office. I remember thinking that, by the grace of God, I would never put anyone else in the same situation. I learned firsthand how painful it was to be the butt of someone's joke or to be hit with a derogatory comment, especially in front of an audience.

A ministerial fellowship works best when ministers generally agree to respect each other and refrain from damaging the ministry of others. Whenever preachers freely criticize and tear down their fellow laborers, whether in their local churches or in organization-wide forums, they weaken the body of Christ that they ought to preserve. On the other hand, sanctions against openness and honest dialogue would be equally wrong. If we are not allowed to speak our minds, we are in danger of becoming cultic or hidebound. Somewhere, between the two views, a neutral ground exists. We must learn how to be truthful—even outspoken—in our remarks yet maintain a mutual respect for one another and avoid attacking and destroying each other.

This ideal is not getting any easier to achieve. When an organization expands, certain stress points inevitably appear. Situations that were manageable twenty years ago take

Respect

much more effort to manage today. For example, as assemblies grow larger, they look less to external fellowship for programs and momentum, thus making the organization work harder to stay relevant. Education and wealth have become more commonplace in our churches, mirroring society at large, and has diminished the need or desire for ministers to defer to traditional centers of authority. Also, greater numbers of ministers gravitate toward groups and subgroups that have always existed. This gravitational pull has been enhanced by modern technological changes that enable people to connect in different ways and forms. We now have conferences within conferences, organizations within organizations, and groups within groups, each generating their own mission statements, setting their own objectives, electing their own leaders, and raising their own funds. Whether we approve or disapprove of these developments is not the point. Our attitudes and actions will always be the point.

Regardless of the various pressures that emphasize our differences, we still have an obligation, in principle, to respect each other. Unfortunately, this is not always the case. Some think that if the preacher in the next town, the next section, or the next district does not believe and preach 100 percent the same as they do, he is fair game. They refuse even to call another minister a *brother* if he deviates from a self-determined set of criteria. With this excuse, they justify making derogatory statements by simply dismissing their target as "the enemy." And, lest anyone think only extremists on one side do this, there are extremists on the opposite side who possess the identical attitude.

The View from the Back of the Pulpit

Positive Communication

Of course, most of us would never single out anyone by name to malign him or her publicly. But some might talk about groups of ministers, mentioning certain things about them, and leave their listeners to draw their own conclusions. I believe that we must take great care in making any remarks, sending emails, writing letters, or posting articles that undermine our fellowship or any minister in particular. We should communicate only in ways that will deliver a positive effect on our organization. Here are a few guidelines that may help.

Is it true? No one who has lived in our nation in recent decades needs to know anything more about spin, innuendo, rumor, and misconstruing facts. A single statement or event can be devastating in the hands of a clever person with an agenda. We should give the benefit of the doubt as long as possible to anyone, especially to a fellow minister. Even if something is true, the context in which it happened may allay harsh judgment.

Are we stretching the truth to make a point? Every pastor has had people in his congregation to embarrass him. In any given service, an individual in rebellion may give a wrong impression of the church as a whole. Also, churches go through difficult times that challenge pastoral leadership. It is particularly unfair for a fellow minister to take advantage of another's misfortune and use it against him.

Does it need to be said at all? Any time we think about criticizing another minister, we need to ask: Am I more interested in looking smug and informed, or am I really trying to be helpful? Am I trying to compensate for my own insecurity? Am I giving life to a story that ought to die? Am I perpetuating a perception of another minister that may be without basis in fact? Actually, I have always found that gossip gets along just fine without my help. And if I can't always avoid hearing some miserable bit of news, I surely don't have to pass it along.

Why does your congregation even need to know? I refuse to harm the congregation I serve with "sanctified" slander. I want them to believe that the UPCI is the greatest organization in the world. I want them to believe that every one of you who reads this article is trustworthy, honorable, faithful to true doctrine, and motivated by love. If they find out otherwise, let it be through someone else. Yes, we have ministers who suffer moral failures. Yes, we have churches that disappoint all of us. Yes, we experience problems between churches and districts. What organization does not? Even so, I believe it is wrong for a UPCI pastor to poison the minds of his people against his organization.

What will the consequences be? When I openly criticize other ministers, I sow seeds of doubt and foster a negative climate in the lives of my listeners. They are likely to share my words with their friends and family, and my indiscretion may ignite a firestorm. The people I pastor have family and friends from Maine to California, from North Dakota to Florida, not to mention cities and towns all over Ohio. Our society is simply too connected and too mobile for us to think criticism won't extend beyond our local churches. Now, widespread access to the Internet exponentially compounds this problem. Ministers have discovered that their DVD or preaching clip recorded through someone's cell phone can wind up on a video file viewed by the world.

The View from the Back of the Pulpit

Furthermore, my people are going to reflect my views. If I make rude and disrespectful remarks from my pulpit about other ministers and churches, those under my leadership will adopt the same feelings. I will end up creating a church full of critics with self-righteous attitudes who constantly scrutinize members of other churches.

Where are your vulnerable areas? Be careful when you enter the fray of open criticism. All of us have an Achilles heel somewhere, and we never know when or by whom it will be exposed. Remember, "For all they that take the sword shall perish with the sword" (Matthew 26:52). Many times, pastors who focus on the perceived shortcomings of others build up a backlog of resentment against themselves. Whenever the dam breaks—and eventually it will—the results can be devastating.

Talk about ideas, not about men. Spend your vital energy addressing the great themes of love, faith, justice, and truth. Dig deeply into the treasure house of Scripture and feed people spiritually enriching manna. Use biblical illustrations to reinforce your points. Your ministry will soar to greater heights by proclaiming a positive message than it ever will by wading into dogfights. Even if you are right about someone, do not allow your tongue or pen to assume the role of God's judgment.

I believe each member of an organization should accept the responsibility to keep it strong. Healthy respect for each other is one good way to carry out that responsibility.

Chapter 8
Shepherds or Sheep Transporters?

Neither as being lords over God's heritage, but being ensamples to the flock (I Peter 5:3).

Tired of being downwind from some unpleasant aromas and having my view blocked, I swung around a muddy sheep trailer on the highway recently and sneaked a peek at the wooly cargo. They didn't seem too happy as the big eighteen-wheeler swayed and they struggled to stay on their feet. Their eyes were wide and their ears lay back against their necks. They may have even been suffering from emotional or psychological damage during their ordeal. The guy driving the rig didn't appear to be too much of a shepherd, either. A typical truck driver, he looked like he just wanted to make his destination point ASAP and unload the smelly freight.

As I recall that scene, I am made to think of the relationship between pastors and saints in churches across the country. David's psalm that speaks of leading the sheep beside the still waters and making them lie down in green pastures

The View from the Back of the Pulpit

sometimes seems far more serene than the real experience. Many times a pastor races through the long week, from Sunday to Sunday, hauling the saints behind him. His greatest hope for the journey is just that no major problems erupt back there in the trailer.

Alas, the dreaded breakdown often happens. The misfortunate shepherd then has to get personally involved, gather the sheep around him, and carry them to the next weekend. Some of the sheep rush him before he can get his door fully open. Some of the more insecure ones hold to his neck in a death grip. Some cling to his back, burrow into his hair, obscure his vision, wiggle around uncontrollably, and demand his attention. Some are way too heavy to carry but they are too immature to know or care. Some get underfoot and cause him to stumble over them. Some test the limits of their freedom and wander to the edges, some are determined to eat poisonous herbs along the fence, some are enamored with the goats on the other side of the fence, and some think the grass is greener over there anyway. Some want painful burrs removed, tender feet cared for, or ears tousled. Others want to play games along the way. Some want the water a little cooler, the grass a little sweeter, and the ground a little softer. When the circumstances are not suitable, they know how to whine and complain until they get their way.

But the sheep are not the only party to the problems. Some shepherds like to stay in the climate-controlled cab, listen to their favorite music, sip their coffee, and roll effortlessly down the turnpike. Some don't like soiling their clothes, handling shovels and rakes, or getting dirt—or worse—under their nails. Some get irritated that the dumb

Shepherds or Sheep Transporters?

animals won't behave properly. They remind the lowly creatures that they know absolutely nothing about driving a truck, reading a map, or passing the test for a chauffeur's license. Some grow testy when the sheep won't obey their clear commands, even though they communicate the commands in shrill tones at top decibel level. They believe the duty of the sheep is to create as little fuss and muss as possible as they head through the week. Sometimes they feel that the weekly beating needs to be more severe. The difference between shepherding and hauling tends to be stark.

Healthy, well-adjusted saints don't need or want the pastor to be their panacea for every sniffle and bad dream. They don't view him as an alter ego, the hand-holder, or the daily arbiter of every decision. As they reach spiritual maturity, they begin to walk and eat on their own. They develop a sense of balance, confidence in their own walk with God, and take on a responsible attitude toward their own tasks. They learn to apply the principles that the pastor teaches, without forming an obsessive/compulsive relationship with the teacher.

> **The wise pastor understands that his job is to help people love God, not become a god to them.**

The wise pastor understands that his job is to help people love God, not become a god to them. He leads them to the water, provides safe passage to the green pastures, and protects them from the predators. He knows that God, not himself, must occupy the center of their lives. He accepts love and honor from people but refuses fawning

The View from the Back of the Pulpit

worship. He guides them through their crisis hours but does not get into the driver's seat to take over their lives. He sees them at their weakest, most vulnerable moments but never takes advantage of those moments to gain leverage or power over them. He edifies without patronizing, heals without obliging, and serves without ingratiating. He walks a fine line between being a shepherd and a sheep transporter.

Heaven is more than an endpoint, and the highway is more than a road—it's a process. And no destination is interwoven more with the journey than is heaven and its travelers en route.

Chapter 9
Surviving Church Storms

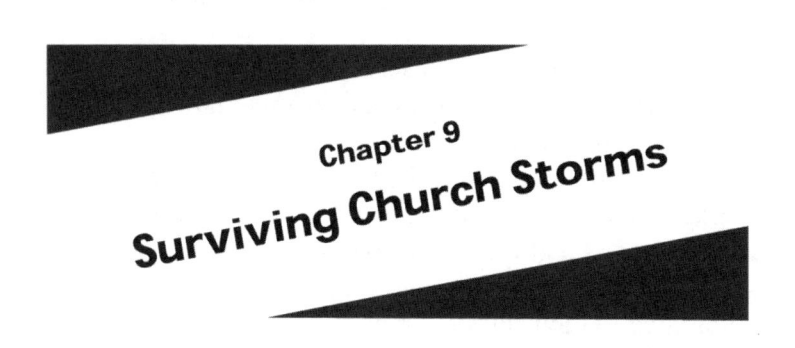

But there be some that trouble you (Galatians 1:7).

The multi-headed church-trouble monster belches fire and smoke out of all its mouths and nostrils. It carves up families, drives wedges between lifelong friends, and destroys souls. All the elements of scandal—money, sex, power, and cover-up—get thrown into the mix. Power struggles, factional disputes, poison pen letters, angry confrontations, and personal threats can turn the picture of tranquility into a murderous maelstrom overnight.

Church trouble can cause unthinkable devastation. Four generations must sometimes pass before the rancor dies down. It triggers such volatile reactions that even writing about it means walking where angels fear to tread.

Granted, troublemakers often sit and wait for opportunities to strike. Most church people, however, are not cold, calculating sleuths who measure every move and launch premeditated strikes. They are innocent people, pure in their motives and passionate about their convictions, and probably have never caused trouble in their lives. In many instances, they found themselves swept into a vortex of misunderstandings, confusing statements, half-truths, and endless recriminations.

Those who launch attacks have often become morally outraged at something and thus refuse to keep quiet. They are convinced that they must expose the leaders and their sympathizers because of some egregious wrongdoing. Once committed to their mission, they rarely can turn back.

For those under attack, there may be no way to sidestep trouble. Their personal reputations may be at stake and they have no choice except to defend their honor. Others have invested so much of their lives into church leadership or church properties that they feel they cannot stay neutral. Still others take a stand on what they see as right, and believe that abandoning their position would be compromising truth. Finally, some remain loyal to the leadership regardless of the cost.

People who have been through church trouble often wish they had either totally stayed out of it or at least handled things differently. Sometimes they admit that they should never have made certain remarks, joined certain factions, or made certain decisions. The rest can only look for lessons in the tragedies. Hopefully, it will never happen to you. If it does, and at the risk of over-simplification, here are some truths and priorities to keep in mind.

Warnings for Church Members

For church members who find themselves involved in church trouble: You and your family must be saved. What have you gained if you jump into the fray and end up losing your family and your own soul? Hatred, bitterness, resentment, and anger are spiritual cancers. If you yield to them, you will suffer deep wounds. Even if you're right, the fight may prove so costly that you may as well have been wrong. Keep the big picture in mind.

Standing for truth does not mean you have to become involved in strife and contention. You not only ruin your witness when you turn to ugliness and strife, but you make things worse. Memorize the fruit of the Spirit and make sure you incorporate them into every aspect of your response to the problem. You can be true to your convictions without compromising the Spirit of Christ.

Do your best to preserve the unity of the church. Churches can survive huge problems if the majority of the people—or at least the pillars of the church—remains united. Despite hurtful losses, don't throw up your hands in despair and abandon the cause. A wounded church has a chance for recovery, but a destroyed church may never rise from the ashes. Most importantly, don't measure any loss in money, buildings, or lands but in eternal souls.

Churches can survive huge problems if the majority of the people—or at least the pillars of the church—remains united. Despite hurtful losses, don't throw up your hands in despair and abandon the cause.

Don't take it personally. People will hurl all kinds of insults at you and put their absolute worst on display to get their way or to be heard. Understand what is going on, let them vent, and then forget about it. Eventually, they will be sorry. Overlook hurt as much as possible.

Support leadership if at all possible. God expects you to honor the spiritual authority in your church. You may not agree with it; some of the things said and done may be ill-advised but you can never justify rebellion. Your first inclination should always be to support the pastor.

If you cannot support the leadership, *do not tear it down!* There is a vast difference between withdrawing support and launching an attack. No matter what a pastor has done, God has neither appointed you nor anyone else to declare war on him. Saul's undoing came at his own hand, not by the hand of David, whom he had grievously wronged.

Do not become someone's pawn. When you deliver the hateful messages of others or fire the bullets that others have made, you make yourself the target. Often, one or two people form the core of the problem. They will use any sympathizer to carry out their wishes.

You don't have to win; the truth does. Over time, this is what usually happens. Get your pride and ego under control. Be willing to take the humble side if it means the salvation of the church and the triumph of the Apostolic message. Only your pride is served if you plant your flag on a pile of ashes and proclaim victory.

The Pastor's Role

A few special notes to pastors: Maintain a good spirit. Of all the people involved in a church problem, the pastor is the only one expected to act like a Christian. Stay upbeat, kind, gentle, and loving. Even in the face of the worst attacks, keep your composure. An angry response, even if it is justified, may be the thing people remember most.

People respond more to perceptions than reality. Don't get mad at them for not trusting you implicitly. Just be prepared to show the real side of the story so as to set everything straight.

Nobody bats a thousand. Regardless of what you do, some people will not respond to your leadership. Even Jesus had Judas. Usually, the people who cause you problems are the very people into whom you have invested most of your time and energy. If they leave, don't let your dreams leave with them. God called you; they didn't.

When the time is right, deal with the problem. The best way to proceed varies from place to place. Much depends on the situation itself. You should make a few phone calls to your elders around the district or nation and get some wise counsel. How you deal with it is your decision, but one thing is certain: don't sweep it under the rug. Don't run from it. Remember that the crisis hour of the present will most likely define your leadership for the future.

If you are wrong, face it. People don't expect you to be perfect, but they do want you to be honest. Their capacity to forgive may be greater than you know. Asking for forgiveness is not a show of weakness.

Get back to your vision. Even as you hurt, you must lead your people into new, positive territory. Don't languish in the shadows of what might have been. You will know it is getting to you if you let the problem dictate every prayer, sermon, and Bible study. If you find yourself wasting hour

The View from the Back of the Pulpit

after hour thinking about it, you're going to make yourself sick and you will negatively affect your church. You must regroup. Reevaluate your position and formulate new plans in keeping with the people who stayed with you and the resources you control. Tomorrow is a new day.

Pastors may not be able to prevent or contain every incident of church trouble. The best thing any of us can do is to maintain our prayer life and let God provide divine direction to help us navigate through the storm. Once the storm hits, our goal should always be to preserve the flock and maintain our personal walk with God. A hundred years from now, should the Lord tarry, that's all that will matter anyway.

A final note for all: There may never be an ultimate win for anyone. This may be the most difficult thing of all to swallow: Accept the fact that the truth may never be fully known, at least in this life. If you keep things stirred up, you will probably engage only in a futile exercise. Review the parable of the tares and the wheat. Prematurely uprooting the evil weeds may inadvertently destroy valuable wheat. Never forget that you do not see the complete picture. Only God sees the hearts, and only He is capable of executing righteous judgment. Be content for God to sort in all out in the end.

Chapter 10
That Vision Thing

*The burden of the valley of vision. . . . For **it is a day of trouble, and of treading down, and of perplexity by the Lord GOD of hosts in the valley of vision**, breaking down the walls, and of crying to the mountains* (Isaiah 22:1, 5; emphasis mine).

Where there is no vision, the people perish (Proverbs 29:18).

And Joseph remembered the dreams which he dreamed of them, and said unto them, Ye are spies; to see the nakedness of the land ye are come (Genesis 42:9).

Then thou scarest me with dreams, and terrifiest me through visions (Job 7:14).

Dreams vs. Visions

Visions and dreams are used interchangeably in the Bible. Both can be either from God or from the flesh. Jacob was a dreamer. Joseph was a dreamer. But even though Peter and Paul had dreams, we do not call them dreamers. We call them visionaries.

The View from the Back of the Pulpit

Dreams seem to be premonitions of the future. Visions seem to be understandings of the future. Dreams wait to be fulfilled. Visions call for action and active faith. But our use of the words *dream* and *vision* today differ from the language of the Bible. Today, *vision* relates more to tomorrow; *dream* relates to yesterday.

> *And it shall come to pass in the last days, saith God, I will pour out of my Spirit upon all flesh: and your sons and your daughters shall prophesy, and your young men shall see visions, and your old men shall dream dreams* (Acts 2:17).

Visions are for the future.
Dreams are for the past.
Dreams focus on what was or what might have been.
Visions focus on what has not happened or what will be.
A dream needs no basis in reality in order to have value.
A vision has value *precisely* because it is based in reality.
A dream needs no connection to the present.
A vision thrives on its connection to the present.
Dreams happen when your eyes are shut.
Visions happen with your eyes wide open.
Everybody can dream.
Vision requires something more.
Dreams may be nothing more than fantasy.
Visions are ventures of faith.
Dreams are cheap.
Visions are expensive.
Unfulfilled dreams can fade without a second thought.
Unfulfilled visions lead to discontent and frustration.

That Vision Thing

When you say, "I will do this or that," you are expressing your vision; when you say, "I will not do this or that," you are also expressing your vision.
You must have a vision for the future. You cannot dream about it.
If you dream about the future, you are treating it as if it were the past.
Dreams deceive the dreamer with a false sense of rest and fulfillment.
Visions demand high energy, commitment, and work.
A dream or a vision: which do you want?

The future will happen whether or not you have a vision. Without a vision, you will perish. With a vision, you will flourish. Which do you want to do, perish or flourish?

Ne Plus Ultra

In Spain, a mountain rises from the bottom of the ocean 1,500 feet above the surface, called the Rock of Gibraltar. Only a little more than five hundred years ago (in history, five hundred years is a very short time) the Spanish government still had carved on the Rock of Gibraltar the words, "Ne Plus Ultra," to protect people from falling off the cliff of a flat world. It means "There is nothing beyond! Stop! Don't go any farther!" When Columbus discovered that the world did not stop at Gibraltar, Spain removed the word "ne." "Ne Plus Ultra" became "Plus Ultra"; there *is* something beyond!

Vision recognizes something exists beyond where you stand!

The View from the Back of the Pulpit

The Vision of Joshua and Caleb

Your vision defines your attitude and action. In Numbers 13:1-33, God told Moses to send spies to explore the land of Canaan that He had bequeathed to the Israelites. Moses recruited twelve men and instructed them to see what the land was like and to assess the strength and numbers of the people who lived there. He especially wanted to know whether the land was fertile. He told them to bring back some produce so he could judge for himself.

The men went but brought back an ambiguous report. The land, they said, "floweth with milk and honey," but powerful giants who inhabited large, fortified cities lived there. Despite Caleb's strong assertion that the Israelites could prevail, ten of the twelve spies were dead-set against it. Fear of failure overwhelmed them. "We were in our own sight as grasshoppers, and so we were in their sight," they cried. Their faith rose no higher than their vision.

Your vision informs your feelings how to feel. When you envision weakness, you make yourself weak. When you envision God's strength, you will be strong.

Negative visions are as contagious as positive ones. When the evil spies' pessimistic report was published throughout Israel, the entire nation began grumbling *en masse* against Moses. They spewed out their bitterness with such fury that they even cursed their deliverance from the bondage of Egypt! An unthinkable scenario developed: they were ready to pick a new leader who would take them back to slavery.

In dramatic fashion, Moses and Aaron fell on their faces before the people to counteract the negative report. Joshua

That Vision Thing

and Caleb then stood up and pled with Israel to change their minds and move forward. They assured everyone that Canaan was a luxuriant and fertile country and that God would give them victory over the inhabitants, even though they seemed like giants. They repeatedly pressed the people not to be afraid of the obstacles before them. Although Israel rejected their plea, dooming the people to wander thirty-eight more years in the wilderness, the vision of Joshua and Caleb never died. It took the passing of a generation, but they saw the walls of Jericho fall.

> **Six Musts of the Vision of Joshua and Caleb:**
> 1. They desired to possess the land.
> 2. They believed they had a right to the land.
> 3. They believed that failure to act was to rebel against the Lord.
> 4. They believed they could defeat the enemy.
> 5. They refused to be ruled by fear.
> 6. They were ready to make their move.

The Bible brims with visionaries. Abraham saw a new land with a new city; Joseph envisioned power and influence; Moses saw deliverance for the Hebrew nation; King David envisioned building a beautiful temple to honor God; his son Solomon envisioned a kingdom that spread over the earth; Peter saw a society free from racial prejudice; Paul envisioned preaching the gospel to every nation. Whether the vision was small, like Dorcas clothing the saints, or vast, like Christ saving the world, nothing significant happened without the force of vision birthing it into existence.

The View from the Back of the Pulpit

Your Vision Is Waiting

A vision for yourself. Start by acting upon your personal vision.

A vision for your family. You don't work on your vision by telling others what to do. You work on your vision by investing yourself into your vision. Put a plan into action that brings reality to your family vision.

A vision for your ministry. What has God called you to do? Notice, I didn't say, "called to be." Too many of us think that to do something we have to be something. You can win souls without thinking of yourself as a soulwinner. You can witness without being a preacher. You can care for people without being a pastor. You can work in ministry without the title or position of minister. Take care of what you do. Who you are will take care of itself.

A vision for your church.
>Envision a loving church.
>Envision a forgiving church.
>Envision a caring church.
>Envision a helping church.
>Envision a participating church.
>Envision a giving church.
>Envision a growing church.

A vision is not "I want this"; a vision is "I see this."
A vision does not say, "If only I had this"; a vision says, "I will get this done."

Going after your vision will not be easy. "For **it is a day of trouble, and of treading down, and of perplexity by**

That Vision Thing

the Lord GOD of hosts in the valley of vision, breaking down the walls, and of crying to the mountains" (Isaiah 22:5, emphasis mine).

These are your musts:
You must desire to take possession of your vision.
You must believe you have a right to your vision.
Failure to act on your vision will be rebellion against the Lord.
You must believe you can defeat the enemy of your vision.
You must refuse to be ruled by fear of your vision.
You must be ready to move toward your vision.

Revisit your dreams. Have they faded and died? Are they forgotten? Turn those dreams into visions. Inject life into your vision. Your vision is worth everything. Your vision is worth dying for. Your vision will forevermore define your life.

Earmarks of the True Visionary

A true visionary

Starts something he cannot finish. . . .
Builds something he cannot control. . . .
Goes places not on the map. . . .
Embraces things not fully understood. . . .
Becomes someone he has never been.

The View from the Back of the Pulpit

You are a true visionary when you are willing to start something you cannot finish. Either your vision is too big for you to finish by yourself, or it will take too long to complete in your lifetime. You need not harvest the glory of a completed task; indeed, it would be absurd to think in terms of personal glory. You are content to sow the seed that puts it all into motion. This is not condoning procrastination or laziness but is a testament to the grand dream.

The founders of the American democracy knew they could not finish their task. Abraham Lincoln did not know the full ramifications of the Emancipation Proclamation. The apostle Peter did not know where the open Gentile door would lead the church. None of them allowed the enormity of their vision to stop them from lighting the fuse.

You are a true visionary when you are willing to go places that are not on the map. You do not seek the charted course. You don't look for a dream previously accomplished. You do not need the security of the known way. You see places others think don't exist; you envision successes that history has not yet recorded; you hear sounds that have not been produced.

Abraham left Ur of the Chaldees, not knowing where he was going. Paul launched his missionary journeys not sure of his destination. Christopher Columbus left "Ne Plus Ultra" on the basis of a dream.

You are a true visionary when you are willing to build something you cannot control. To see your success skyrocket far beyond that which you anticipated excites you. You see something so big, so wildly successful that you actually become immaterial to the end result. You realize that the thing you create may render you obsolete,

That Vision Thing

but you would rather be eclipsed by your own success than marinate in mediocrity. It was said of Jesus, "Because zeal for Your house has eaten me up" (Psalm 69:9, NKJV). A Bay Area analyst, Robert Warburg, jokes, "[Bill Gates's] greatest fear is that some kid will brew up the next killer app in his garage in Kenosha, and Microsoft won't own it!" You are willing to turn the control over to God.

You are a true visionary when you are willing to embrace something you do not fully understand. Wilbur and Orville Wright did not understand the impact that their flying machine would have on worldwide transportation when they became airborne at Kitty Hawk, North Carolina. Bill Gates did not understand all the implications the nascent computer field would have for the world when he designed Microsoft Windows™ in his garage. Frank Ewart and R. E. McAlister did not fully understand all there was to know about Oneness theology when they began preaching it in the early twentieth century. Yet all of them took the leap because they were convinced it was the right thing to do.

The visionary suspects that there are endless possibilities in his idea or dream. He boldly lets that truth go wherever it wants to go. To insist on understanding every minuscule detail of the truth would abort the birth before the baby ever has a chance to say hello to the world.

You are a true visionary when you are willing to become who you have never been before. Securely locked within our insular definitions, most of us shut down when life tries to transition us into a new calling. When innovative ideas threaten to inflict too great a change on our status quo, our crusty old wineskins start to burst. We would rather say no and be safe than say yes and be infinitely

The View from the Back of the Pulpit

better or set off vast changes on the human landscape.

Abe Lincoln started out as a farm boy, but he saw himself as a businessman, a surveyor, a postman, a lawyer, a congressman, and then as President of the United States. Neil Armstrong, from his beginnings in the small town of Wapakoneta, Ohio, started out as a navy aviator, then a test pilot, a backup astronaut, then the first man on the moon.

John Nickerson, while a UPCI missionary in Nigeria, believed that the African continent stood ready to be set ablaze with revival fires—not only for the outpouring of the Holy Spirit but also to receive the revelation of the oneness of God and baptism in Jesus' name. He shared his vision with his many partners in missions, and he readily admitted that the river of his vision could overflow its banks. Even now, as momentum builds, hundreds of pastors with roots outside of Apostolic circles have already been baptized. His passion represents the earmarks of a true visionary.

> **Bring me men to match my mountains,**
> **Bring me men to match my plains,**
> **Men with empires in their purpose**
> **And new eras in their brains.**
> —*Sam Foss*

I Am a Person of Vision!

I have been a pew-warmer, a fence-walker, a spectator for too long.
I am getting up, getting right, and getting going.
I may not see the entire picture, but I see my picture.
I can't try everything, but I will try something.

That Vision Thing

I may fail trying, but I won't fail to try.
I may not make much on my investment, but I won't bury my talent in the ground.
I will act even though I receive no thanks in return.
I will pray and leave the answer up to God.
I will witness and leave the response up to the person.
I will smile even though no one smiles back.
I will give because it is right, not because I expect something in exchange for my gift.
I am blood bought, Word taught, and miraculously wrought.
I am divinely created, Spirit filled, God called and Heaven sent.
I am saved by grace, programmed to succeed, wired for power, and mission-oriented.
God is my commander-in-chief.
Jesus is my Savior.
My pastor is my coach.
The Bible is my blueprint.
The Holy Ghost is my guide.
The world is my mission field.
I will be immune to criticism, unbowed by critics, unmoved by suffering, and unashamed of the gospel.
I will obey like Noah, sacrifice like Abraham, fight like David, pray like Daniel, be patient like Job, see God's greatness like Isaiah, weep like Jeremiah, preach like Peter, and reach out like Paul.
I have nothing greater to live for and nothing better to die for.
I am a person of vision!

—J. Mark Jordan

Chapter 11
Walk with Me

Walk worthy of the vocation wherewith ye are called (Ephesians 4:1).

Take the moccasins. Let's walk. You probably won't get used to the path and you won't want to go every place it leads, but pastors don't choose their paths or pick the scenery along the way. Sometimes the path winds back on itself, as if you didn't get enough the first time. I can only say that if you walk far enough, you'll see everything you need to see.

If you dare, walk with me into the surgical waiting room. A family has been sitting there, full of hope that everything would be fine. Now, they've learned that their mother didn't make it through the surgery. A volcano of emotion erupts—from wailing and screaming to shrill prayers and bitter expressions—striking fear even into the hearts of bystanders. The grieving family immediately looks to me with imploring eyes, expecting me to provide instant answers to their questions. The best I can do is bring a calming influence into the chaos.

The View from the Back of the Pulpit

Walk with me into my tension-filled office. A man has just confessed a lurid affair, and his wife sits in stunned disbelief. After a few minutes, her anger and hurt boils into a tearful rage; then she collapses into painful self-recriminations. Back and forth it goes. Hours later, they quietly leave, still not knowing whether or not they can make it as a married couple any longer. The strange emptiness of unrequited pain gathers into the corners of the room.

Next, we can take some tokens for the vending machines, plus the clothes on our backs, but that's it. We enter a stark, institutional-looking visiting room. The man in a light blue shirt with dark blue trousers comes to see us, a forced smile in the place of his usual wide grin. He just went before the parole board three weeks prior. Admittedly a convicted felon, he's eight years into a ten-to-twenty-five, but they denied him an early release for no reason except that they could. Each inmate they keep brings thousands of dollars from the state into the correctional system. There is a chance he may have to do the maximum. He wants to know why God allowed this to happen.

Returning, we walk by a courtroom. A judge is giving his less-than-satisfactory reasons why he gave the kids to the other parent, the one whom we know filed for custody to spite the ex-spouse. We also know, intuitively, that the children are headed for a life of neglect and bad influence. We can hardly bear the anguish we see in the parent's face. Again, the questions arise, and some answers are expected.

In the back of the sanctuary, after service has been

Walk with Me

dismissed, listen with me to a man pouring out his heart over the loss of his job and his inability to take care of his family. The bank is about to foreclose on his mortgage, he is three months behind on all his bills, and he has no idea when his first unemployment check will arrive in the mail. He wants answers, and money, quickly.

I know you're tired, but before you go home, we need to listen to a teenage girl tell us that she thinks she is pregnant, a troubled woman relate the story of horrific nightmares invading her sleep the last few weeks, a man who doesn't know what to do about his son who is strung out on cocaine, a wife whose husband doesn't want to come to church any longer, a woman who feels unbearable pressure from her family for failing to meet their expectations, an elderly widow whose son is taking advantage of her financially, a five-year-old boy who wants me to pray because his mommy and daddy are getting a divorce, a young mother who wants to know if demons can torment her children, a man who is about to lose his business, and another man who is thinking of moving to another state.

Walk with me to my library where I try to submerge myself into research and study. I know you thought there would be whole days where I could browse books, read journals, feast on Scripture, and pray at leisure. What a life that would be! But phone interruptions and obligations just remembered break up the few hours set aside to work. When I do get back to the books, there's the pressure of a deadline or agonizing over what to preach to people who desperately need help.

Okay, I'll let you go today, but tomorrow we'll

The View from the Back of the Pulpit

walk some more. We'll talk to the church secretary about the unexpected utilities expenses and hefty increases in the insurance premiums. We'll talk to the maintenance man about replacing the big lawn mower, and the major repairs needed on the van. After that, we'll travel to a neighboring town and sit with the pastor who is about to give it up because of church trouble that threatens his congregation.

Did you think we would walk to exotic vacations, fishing trips, and golf outings? Even if we do, be prepared to leave town later and return home earlier than we wanted to. You thought you could sleep in most mornings, too? Sorry to disappoint you. You might not leave the house early, but you'll still be up before the sun—writing, reading, studying, and treasuring any uninterrupted time afforded you. Taking phone calls and replying to emails poke holes in your mornings as well.

Walk with me softly through delicate encounters where a wrong word may foment a crisis. Sometimes, an encouraging word will suffice, but usually I search my soul to give a word of direction, enlightenment, comfort, or exhortation. Walk boldly with me into demons' lairs and lions' dens, or walk carefully with me into hotbeds of malicious rumors or into darkened rooms where infinite sadness prevails. Walk with me into emergency rooms, funeral parlors, neonatal units, psychiatric wards, nursing homes, lawyers' offices, and police stations. Walk with me into board rooms where men of God earnestly discuss some doctrinal error or where they painfully decide the fate of a comrade who has fallen into sin.

Walk with Me

Sit with me and stare out the window of a coffee shop. Black. No cream or sugar. Wheat toast, please. Commiserate with me as I breathe a long, low sigh. You know, I'm not the man for the job. Others would be a blazing success where monuments to my failures stand in silent mockery to me. Anyone . . . I don't know. . . . See that guy over there? He could probably do a better job than me. Look at these help-wanted ads. Think I could do that? I wonder . . . but it's just this call . . . this unrelenting call. . . . My cell phone just vibrated. It's the hospital . . . again. Leave an extra tip. The newspaper? No, someone else can have it . . . maybe that guy over there.

Just when we think we've had enough, the scenery changes. Walk with me into the arms of a loyal saint who loves preachers. He hands me a card and a check, not a lot but enough to soothe the agitations of a tough week. I feel the hand of a deacon laid on my shoulder and hear him remind me that he's praying for me. We stop by a pew long enough for a saint to tell me that my sermon was an answer to her prayers. I look over and establish eye contact with a man I know has been going through hell itself. He gives me a thumbs-up and mouths the word, "Thanks!"

Schedule a baby dedication for some parents whose pride is bursting out all over. Go over some wedding plans with an excited young couple who want to do things the right way. Laugh in the vestibule with some crazy guys who read a new joke over the Internet. Rejoice with the lady who was troubled by nightmares as she declares victory in Jesus' name. Glorify God for a

The View from the Back of the Pulpit

full house at the last service. Breathe a sigh of relief when the woman whose marriage was on the rocks tells you that things are working out. Feel even more relief when the secretary tells me that the bills are paid with money left over. Praise God with the entire church as a young mother reports that the MRI on her five-year-old son shows no trace of a cancerous brain tumor.

Linger awhile with me at the altar, and listen to a young man speak in a glorious new language as the Spirit baptizes him. Help me pray with the middle-aged couple who kneels in a renewed commitment to God, so needed after wandering in a spiritual drought. Sense the sweet release of sins a dad must feel as he rises from the baptismal waters, his bearded face awash in heaven's glow. Watch tears of repentance flow down the cheeks of a teenaged girl who got herself into trouble. Stay long enough to see her parents hug her, wipe her moist eyes, and tell her they love her.

Maybe you've now walked far enough to see what you needed to see. Sometimes it's up, sometimes it's down, but the path keeps unfolding. I cannot yet say whether it all evens out. Every day, I just venture into the great unexplored, accompanied by both dread and anticipation. You can go back to what you were doing. I've got "miles to go before I sleep."

Chapter 12
Who Are These People?

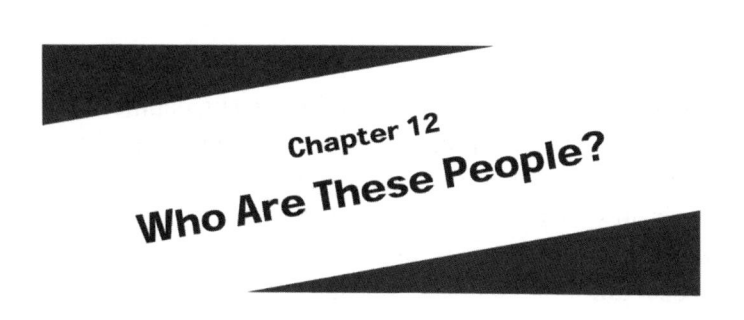

Church Life in the New Millennium: The new generation of churchgoers presents challenges to pastors and leaders that differ significantly from the stereotypes of the past. The old assumptions no longer work. We need to take a fresh look at the way we handle the people who are caught up in the sweeping social and cultural revolution. The leadership of the Holy Spirit has become more necessary now than ever. Let's look at the problem from the perspective of the church.

Returned Prodigals. Those who left the church many years ago and have just returned have unique needs and cannot be lumped together with everyone else. Do not assume that they "know the score." Understand that they have had little or no spiritual growth for years. They resemble Rip Van Winkle, who woke up from a twenty-year nap. When they come back, therefore, they have highly idealized and naive expectations of themselves and others. If they left church as a child or a teenager, they still have a child's or a teenager's view of the church. Also, those who enjoyed a relatively high status before they left may never achieve the same level. The initial enthusiasm of their return may fade quickly when it dawns on them that they forfeited their previous esteem. First, make them aware that their salvation is more important than anything else. After a reasonable passage of time, they may once again be qualified for advancement. These things have to be decided on a case-by-case basis.

Spiritual Stepchildren. Not all move-ins are the same. Some have relocated to your city because of a job situation. Some are going to school, joining the military, or are adjusting to changing family circumstances. Others, however, are refugees from church fights or have suffered embarrassing problems that forced them to leave and go elsewhere. The protocols of the transfers are another story, but after they come, the immediate concern must focus on the welfare of the move-in. In their new church environment, they experience many of the same emotions that stepchildren have in real life. They do not respond to authoritarian leadership. They must be persuaded, affirmed, and won over.

The Plugged-In. The local church no longer serves as the only source of religious information for today's members. The Internet has revolutionized communication and networking. People have access to multiple sources of church-world news, theological views, newsletters, special interest groups, chat rooms, Web sites, and forums that disseminate ideas from every doctrinal position imaginable. Maintaining control in the new millennium has become a far more difficult task than

Who Are These People?

ever before. Church leaders must continue to educate themselves about the subjects that much of their congregation knows like the backs of their hands. Those who refer to hippies, discos, and other outdated terms of the past alienate their younger audience. We cannot ignore the fact that a ready-made argument against nearly everything we preach and teach exists in the minds of churchgoers. The more dated and out-of-touch church leaders seem, the less influence they wield.

The Resident Analysts. Our demand for high commitment and separation from the world meets with high resistance from a certain segment of people who continue to attend church but never fully comply with the teachings and standards. Due to their family ties or friendships, they remain a part of the social fabric of the church. They may give financial support, help with building projects, or perform certain services like driving a bus or mowing a lawn. This status gives them an informal voice in the congregation. They have deep, underlying issues, however, that surface from time to time through criticism or blatant nonconformity. They analyze much of the pulpit offerings through carnal or secular opinions. Use them where you can, but continue to appeal to their conscience. Offset their influence with a powerful and persuasive ministry.

The Spiritual Singles. People with unsaved spouses have long been a part of church life, going all the way back to New Testament times. Many of them are extremely sensitive to comments, sermons, or programs that emphasize family unity or spirituality. They battle with feelings of resentment, jealousy, and even depression. Address their concerns and needs without making them feel they are second-class citizens. They don't necessarily expect church programs to be shaped to accommodate them, but they must know that the leadership recognizes their unique problems. Consider special classes, support groups, or other activities designed to make them feel included.

Fractured Families. My kids, your kids, our kids, my ex's kids, your ex's kids, and maybe someone else's kids, all living under the same roof, can create severe strain on families that impacts church life. Custody rules force many kids to spend alternate weekends with the other parent, often causing great confusion in parenting rules and undermining authority. If we stereotype family structures as being predominantly nuclear, those caught in these anomalies either feel stigmatized or irrelevant. People with formerly atypical backgrounds are more and more becoming mainstream. But what if it seems as though we are losing our Apostolic culture when we so much as acknowledge that these problems exist? Granted, today's behaviors mess up our tidy sandbox, but we cannot change the social landscape with a wave of the hand. Even as Jesus "must needs go through Samaria," a cultural nightmare for orthodox Jews, we must make every effort to reach people where and how we find them.

Adult Adolescents. The average age of people leaving the confines of home has crept up in recent decades. Many men and women are in their middle or late twenties before they get out on their own. Are they still a part of the youth group? Should they be expected to

Who Are These People?

behave responsibly and assume positions in the church? We cannot take for granted that they simply ought to grow up without speaking specifically to their status. They are somewhere in between ministering and needing to be ministered to. This group holds tremendous potential for the present and the future. Wise leaders, in an exercise of faith, will show them respect before it has been totally earned.

The Educated. As long as the people with an alphabet of letters after their names were on the outside, we could get away with lambasting the pointy-headed intellectuals. No more. Society's emphasis on education has put many college graduates in our congregations. It changes the way our congregations perceive us, and it must change the way we communicate with them. We will continue to insult the educated at our own peril.

High Talent/Low Commitment. Talented people who populate our pews need more than just to be upbraided for their lack of commitment. The challenges we give them must be commensurate with their superior abilities. They may be more bored than backslidden. The modern milieu of complicated living has imposed higher demands on ministering to people than ever before, forcing us to understand the nuances of leadership. Church leaders need to become students of motivation. People don't do things today just because. They will respond if they can be motivated. Don't leave the high-tech tractor in the barn while you stubbornly continue plowing behind the old gray mare.

The Wealthy. Monied people can be either a great blessing to a church or the source of huge problems.

The View from the Back of the Pulpit

The reason is that, in the minds of many, money equals power. The rich may think that their judgment is worth more than that of others leading them or expect preferential treatment. Much could be said about dealing with the wealthy, but it should be abundantly clear to all that no one can buy influence in the church. Be grateful for larger gifts and acknowledge those who give them, but reserve honor for spiritual attributes like faithfulness, participation, and spirituality.

The Special Interest Groups. The list is long: prophecy enthusiasts, doctrine gurus, theology junkies, worship extremists, music connoisseurs, neat-freaks, standard nitpickers, finance fanatics, political maniacs, liturgical perfectionists, caring-for-the-unfortunate devotees, church building zealots and a host of other offshoots of single-issue saints. They only care about their pet peeve or personal obsession. The problem is that they often succeed in redirecting the total church program into servicing their narrow area and letting everything else go. If you can, put them in charge of their special interest; it may help scratch their itch. If not, preach moderation and the big picture. Above all, remember that the mission of the church represents the broadest objective possible. We cannot afford any diversions that will effectively shut down that mission.

Full-time Pastors and Part-time Saints. People who may not fully utilize their own ministry gifts often consider the pastor to be at their beck and call. He is the servant of the church and therefore must be kept busy. They want him to pay so-and-so a personal visit, read a book that they think will help him, watch a video or

Who Are These People?

DVD that just inspired them, start a new class for an elective series, serve as an on-call counselor who is available for big or little talks 24/7, and do a myriad of other minuscule tasks that they've thought of. They would like to do more for God, but they just don't have time. They have full-time jobs. Part-time saints need to be reminded of the pastor's overwhelming responsibility to direct the total church program. The spiritual myopia of many church members today ensnares too many pastors and church leaders. They constantly have to pare down their vision to squeeze it into the narrow scope of their followers.

In-House Divorcees. Unfortunately, it is becoming more common for couples in the church to get a divorce but continue to attend the same assembly. They often sit on opposite sides of the sanctuary and either glare at or frostily ignore each other. If they have children, it compounds the problem. Over time, the rest of the congregation can usually adjust to the situation. What makes the bad situation worse, however, is if they spread their bitter complaints to others and expect them to take sides. The pastor must play the role of pastor to both of them, but he must not allow their anger to destroy the unity of the church. It is vital for a truce to be enforced, especially on church grounds. Sometimes, only the wisdom of Solomon and the leadership of the Holy Ghost can get us through these situations.

Unwed Mothers. Despite the fact that society generally accepts them without the former stigma, unwed mothers still feel awkward in church circles. The point here is not to cover all the bases but to remind us the church remains the best refuge for these girls who now have enormous complications in their lives. We have a difficult balancing act in treating the girl with love yet not appearing to condone her wrong. Further, we must be extremely careful not to shun one girl for an unwanted pregnancy and then accept another because of her family connections or other circumstances that look like raw favoritism. If we are truly to validate our stand against abortion, we must be prepared to shoulder the alternative with love and forgiveness.

Societal Misfits. Felons, parolees, AIDS victims, social disease carriers, and sexual predators are becoming increasingly common in our society, but due to our emphasis on outreach to jails, prisons, and persons with addictions, we are seeing more of them in our churches. In addition, homosexuals, transvestites, and transgendered persons may indeed be sitting on our pews, sometimes without the knowledge of church leaders. One of the major concerns pastors have is preserving the family atmosphere of the church and making parents feel secure in bringing their children. At the same time, we have a moral and scriptural obligation to minister to people who have gone to the depths of sin. We do have to guard against predators who come among us to exploit children and vulnerable persons. I personally think the pastor needs to inform a number of people in the congregation about a potential problem so they can help him keep an eye out for suspicious situations. If ever we needed the guidance of the Holy Spirit, we need it now.

Chapter 13
Communication: Beyond the Basics

And this I speak for your own profit (I Corinthians 7:35).

Communication rests on the three-legged stool of the sender, the receiver, and the message itself. Beyond this deceptively simple framework, however, other factors exist which complicate the process. Take the caller ID feature on our phones, for example, or the direct path from the mailbox to the wastebasket to dispose of junk mail. Or the spam folder on our Internet browsers. Or the glances we give to the tabloids in the checkout line. All these testify to the complexities of modern communication. We send selected messages to selected recipients, we only tolerate certain kinds of message content, and we accept messages only from certain senders. In our society of information overload, few communicators get a free pass into our ears, eyes, and minds.

The signature message sent by church leadership

The View from the Back of the Pulpit

consists of much more than sermons, lessons, talks, phone calls, letters, faxes, email, promotional campaigns, newsletters, or any other form of communication. It must also be framed in terms of organizational structure, philosophy of management, departmental goals, human factors, and leadership styles. All communication filtering through these elements are not independent from them but, instead, actually become shaped by them. As a river is affected by the topography through which it flows, so too the boundaries, barriers, and general environment through which communication flows bend and shape its substance and effectiveness.

Communication Philosophy

A philosophy is a broad theme that underlies and gives meaning to a way of life. A church, like all organizations, operates with certain basic philosophies, whether written or unwritten, intended or unintended, arbitrary or based on consensus. What kind of philosophy should govern your church administration? Four basic needs become clear in answering this question: 1) Improving the organizational structure and decision-making processes. 2) Shifting toward a teamwork concept that optimizes human resources. 3) Changing the managerial style from "line authority" to more participation and empowerment. 4) Creating a general climate of openness and responsiveness. Let's examine each of these areas.

Organizational Structure. An age-old controversy posits whether form follows function or function follows form. While the proponents of these two schools of thought remain poles apart, they do agree that each has an effect upon the other. Ideally, an organization builds a structure that will be most compatible with its operations. Usually, the by-laws stipulate the church's structure. Some of the structure and much of the administrative work, however, may be determined by pastoral preference. This gives the pastor latitude to make changes that will significantly impact communication efficiency.

An inefficient structure causes problems in communications that may be both serious and difficult to identify. First, bottlenecks may exist which delay the speed of decision-making. Second, there may be redundancy in some communication routes which direct communications along parallel paths or force them to double back for second approvals. Third, job descriptions of all administrative and departmental personnel may be obsolete and must undergo periodic updating. (When you update job descriptions, recall that the strategic significance of any individual's portfolio must be commensurate with his position. As a rule of thumb, a person should do what he alone can and must do, based on his position and authority, but not what may easily be assigned to others.) Fourth, the pastoral staff may want to explore some alternative methods of discipling and ministering to saints. This may involve new convert assignments, allowing some decentralization for limited decision-making power to the lay ministers, and policy review.

Teamwork. One of the most powerful concepts to

sweep the corporate world in the last two decades is that of teamwork. Teamwork has been described as "the ability to work together toward a common vision; the ability to direct individual accomplishment toward organizational objectives; the fuel that allows common people to attain uncommon results." Conceptually, teamwork permits the organization to tap into the optimal potential that resides within its human resources. While every member of the team does not possess identical abilities and talents, through teamwork every member can contribute his best, which will propel the organization toward its objectives.

Teamwork rests upon several crucial givens. First, each team member must be *informed* about the progress of the whole. Second, each member must be *trained* or coached to maximize his performance. Third, each member must fully understand the *role* he plays in the organizational success. Fourth, each member must enjoy a reciprocal *affirmation* of value and worth with his leaders and his peers. Finally, each team member must share in the rewards of success. **Caution:** Teamwork is a total concept that relies on all the components to be in place to work. *Do not implement it partially or selectively and still expect to achieve the desired results.*

Managerial Style. The military modeled the management style that most organizations copied until the recent past. In the military, power concentrated at the top flows downward through a highly defined chain of command. The brass dispenses information on a "need to know" basis, they grant limited decision-making power to subordinates, and they require each element in

Communication: Beyond the Basics

the chain to operate within a set of rigid parameters.

The beauty of the military bureaucracy lies in its simplicity. It is a style that eliminates confusion, ensures that each person knows exactly what he can or cannot do, and gets things done quickly and efficiently, at least in theory. But the efficiency of the military managerial apparatus is also its greatest problem. Officers operate with controlling authority; people within the system become numbers; policies are enforced without regard to their effectiveness; procedures are followed that were devised for different times and under different circumstances; and conformity to rules gets rewarded more than actual results. Leaders demand that subordinates follow SOP even though the consequences are disastrous. Thus we have the wry observation that "the operation was a success, but the patient died."

In recent decades, this autocratic style has been gradually replaced by a greater emphasis on participation and empowerment. Executives still maintain final authority and decision-making power, but they provide much greater latitude for everyone in the organization to make their ideas heard. The new executive style sets up dyads, work-groups, project matrices, and teams that do not just pay lip service to participation but build it into the actual administrative process. In addition, today's executives are more willing to empower their subordinates to do the jobs they are assigned to do. They confer the authority commensurate with the responsibility that the job demands.

The participatory style of management has its problems. Multiple options can complicate the process, clarity may be sacrificed, longstanding procedures get challenged, and one-man control is no longer possible. Yet the end result stimulates the organization in a profound and positive way. People feel valued, their ideas become consequential, their ownership of organizational goals grow, and the entire church morale gets a huge boost.

How does managerial style impact communication? Ted Engstrom and Ed Dayton have some useful words in their book, *The Art of Christian Management*. They identify five different kinds of leadership styles: 1) Bureaucratic, 2) Permissive, 3) Laissez-faire, 4) Participative, and 5) Autocratic. They describe each style and show what each kind of leader values most.

The *bureaucratic* leader believes strongly in rules and regulations; hence, his communications will issue directives or underscore existing ones. The *permissive* leader wants everyone (including himself) to feel good; thus, he avoids confrontation and conflict in his communications. The *laissez-faire* leader believes that the organization will run itself with little or no interference; his communications will be infrequent and vague. The *participatory* leader believes in working together with people and sharing decisions and goals; he will communicate as much as he can to give his subordinates sufficient information to do their work. Finally, the *autocratic* leader assumes that people will only do what they are told to do and that he knows what is best; thus, his communications will seem like pronouncements which discourage innovation. Communication grows out of the style or philosophy that the leadership embraces.

Communication: Beyond the Basics

Leadership styles may vary widely within the church itself and are often as diverse as individual personalities. Church leadership should begin an in-service educational process that will give leaders the background and tools to 1) evaluate themselves and their own styles, 2) familiarize themselves with current thinking in the field of leadership and management, and 3) show them how changes may be made to increase their effectiveness as leaders. Seminars, video courses, on-line resources, and professional consultants along with books and CDs are all available to facilitate this effort.

Organizational Climate. Geophysically, climate is a function of heat, cold, wind, and humidity. Crops, herds, and industry prosper or wither, depending upon the climate. Climate also determines the comfort levels of the population. In the organizational environment, the climate is a composite of attitudes, personalities, values, leadership styles, and general feelings. A good climate produces favorable results and people will be comfortable working there. In a mediocre or poor climate, the results will not reach their full potential and people will express their discomfort. Achieving a good climate will not happen without some deliberate policy decisions implemented to lead the way.

Everything that happens in church leadership should invite inspection and examination of the whole body. Some discrimination, of course, must be applied. The process of communication must start with the decision about what needs to be communicated. If wrong choices are made here, no amount of quality or slickness can

The View from the Back of the Pulpit

compensate. Usually, personal problems in the lives of members are exempted from such open disclosure. Certain events, however, do impinge upon the relationship between the leadership and laity. Anything that has the potential to threaten this relationship needs to be communicated. Good news is easy to talk about. Bad news often gets officially buried, but, unfortunately, it enjoys many unofficial resurrections. It can eventually create a worse situation than it would have had it been aired from the start. An open climate fosters good will and trust throughout the organization. When that happens, programs, projects, and cooperation put forward by church leaders will be received with the same amount of openness.

Chapter 14
You Can't Just Change One Thing

For the priesthood being changed, there is made of necessity a change also of the law (Hebrews 7:12).

While visiting Moscow to play the Russians in the historic Summit Series of 1972, the Canadian hockey team was assigned a room in an elegant hotel, which they suspected had been bugged: "We searched the room for microphones," Phil Esposito recalled. "In the center of the room, we found a funny-looking, round piece of metal embedded in the floor, under the rug. We figured we had found the bug. We dug it out of the floor and heard a crash beneath us. We had released the anchor to the chandelier in the ceiling below."

Change has consequences. Predictably unpredictable, change permits something else to happen, which allows for something else to happen, which allows . . . ad infinitum. "For the want of a nail, the shoe was lost. For the want of the shoe . . ." Call it the domino effect, the can of worms, the chain reaction, the slippery slope,

The View from the Back of the Pulpit

or opening Pandora's Box, but the slightest change in nearly any aspect of life can precipitate a flurry of succeeding changes that astounds the changer, the changee, and nearly everyone else. A familiar maxim holds that nature hates a void, so when any change in procedure, routine, or thought system takes place, an opening automatically appears to permit other forces to act.

Look at history. King George III slapped excise taxes on the colonies and ignited the American Revolution. Germany elected Hitler to restore its national pride, and he plunged the world into WWII. Gorbachev instituted "glasnost," which arguably led to the demise of the Soviet Union. In the Bible, Solomon married foreign wives and sold Israel into idolatry. Simon Peter dared to preach to Cornelius and opened the entire Gentile population to the gospel. In each case, the person or group who precipitated the event probably had no clue of the vast consequences inherent in their minor change. They just wanted to change one little thing.

> **Change bears children—and grandchildren. Change redefines who we are and what we do.**

Change produces pressure on some and relieves pressure on others. Change intimidates some and emboldens others. Change bears children—and grandchildren. Change redefines who we are and what we do. And it does not matter the size of the change. In time, subtle changes can trigger huge reactions. Moreover, most reactions to change are largely unanticipated at the be-

You Can't Change Just One Thing

ginning, develop under the radar during the process, and usually occur unintentionally. Some scholars have labeled it "the law of unintended consequences."

In the church context, people fear, fight, or favor change in almost every facet of behavior. Little wonder. Church culture is so rife with traditional practices that, like a giant helium-filled balloon, it constantly floats up before the congregation as a fat target for change. Something as simple as singing attracts vociferous critics and equally hyped-up defenders. Will we sing new songs or old ones? Will they be fast or slow? Will we clap on the on-beat or off-beat? Will we lean toward rock or country? Will the drums and guitars dominate, or will we purr with the dulcet strains of the Hammond C3? Will we bang or ban the tambourines? And did someone mention the lyrics?

Trends in the way churches now operate deviate significantly from norms once thought to be set in stone. Many congregations have altered their entire organizational structure. Pastors' roles have shifted, dramatically in some cases, to accommodate shared responsibilities and group ministry. Organizational charts feature dotted lines to positions and personnel that were never before part of the conventional decision-making process. Authority flows deeper and broader than ever before. New titles, new ministries, and new objectives have sprouted up to reflect the changes. Other departures from the past procedures include moving from morning to afternoon services, from Sunday school to Wednesday evening school, from "church" to "center," from count to no count, from Bible study to preaching

The View from the Back of the Pulpit

or worship services, from the King James Version to the NEB, NKJV, NIV, or TLB, from corporate services to small group meetings, from pastel blouses and solid ties to choir robes, from white shirts and ties for the preacher to open or cleric collars, from sermons to skits, from audio tapes to CDs or DVDs, from yellow pages to Web sites, from committees to teams, from stained glass to Fresnel lenses with colored gels.

Two broad categories define change: inside the box and outside the box. Changes inside the box pose little or no threat to the church culture, even though they may imperil individuals in their jobs or assignments. They involve changing carpet or paint color, choir directors or Sunday school teachers, or buildings and locations. Of course, disagreements often arise even with minor changes because opinions and tastes vary, but they seldom erupt into revolt or mass defection. They occur within the accepted and expected practices that congregations have followed for many years. Most people realize that when Brother Jones gets up in his eighties, he may have to be replaced on the ushering staff, or when Sister Smith's arthritis keeps her from climbing onto the organ bench, she may have to relinquish her job as the main organist. That's life.

But it's the bigger changes, the ones outside the box, that shake the church's universe. Jesus revolutionized His world by daring to venture outside the box of Judaistic orthodoxy. Toppling the money-exchangers' tables, conversing with the woman of Samaria, healing on the Sabbath day, and boldly proclaiming Himself to be God were neither expected nor accepted. Of course,

You Can't Change Just One Thing

Jesus did not provoke or lead change out of a rebellious attitude or hunger for power. He was not an opportunist responding to a restless citizenry that was clamoring for change to get a piece of the pie. Jesus led change because His world had perverted truth, because the needs of the common man were no longer served by the religious hierarchy, and, most importantly, because the time had come for full salvation to be revealed. He did not savagely destroy a religion out of anger. He reconnected lost mankind back to a greater truth.

The changes Jesus made grew out of omniscience. We have no such advantage. We must approach change with far greater caution and forethought, precisely because we do not know what may result from any given change. For example, let's consider a simple change like switching service times on Sunday from two services, one in the morning and one in the evening, to one afternoon meeting. To those who have grown accustomed to a morning and evening service, two blocks of time are now opened to them that were never before available. What might they now do, where might they now go, or with whom might they now associate during these time slots that had always previously been taken? Let's further consider the repercussions of eliminating Bible study for preaching and worship services. When will a serious, in-depth study of Scripture happen? Will the Scripture used in sermons be enough to meet the need? Will slacking on comprehensive Bible teaching change the rate and level of spiritual maturity?

The spring in which Mel Gibson's movie, *The Passion*, debuted, a minister asked me about going to see it.

The View from the Back of the Pulpit

Here are some excerpts from the reply I sent.

"The principle is 'sow the the wind and reap the whirlwind.' When we agree to something that fundamentally changes our position, we will be forced to accept the consequences. Those consequences are not tit-for-tat, blow for blow, but they increase exponentially on the return . . . wind to whirlwind. One movie means other movies . . . other movies mean many movies . . . many movies mean any movies. Movies, accordingly, exert tremendous cultural, spiritual, and lifestyle pressures on people. After a while, movies are no longer the problem . . . but the changes they introduce to their audiences become the greater problem. For example, some denominational historians have charted a shift toward worldliness in a certain major denomination from a certain point in time that coincided with their consent to go see *The Cross and the Switchblade* back in the sixties. Afterwards, many of their preachers rued the day when they opened that floodgate.

"There is an old saying that you can't put the genie back in the bottle once it has been released. We need to use extreme caution in giving our blessing to something that has the potential to cause a meltdown in our holiness culture. How does that happen? Easily . . . much too easily. 'It looks good . . . let's do it!' That may be all it takes. If our congregations see inconsistency in their leadership, we lose credibility. The younger generation is especially vulnerable to worldly pressure. We cannot afford to waver for their sake."

At the same time, there can be no question that we often need serious changes. Without change, we die.

You Can't Change Just One Thing

This includes out-of-the-box changes that fundamentally alter the way we operate. We make a huge mistake, however, if we change things in a hurry, failing to notice the interdependent nature of all the elements involved. This opens us up for disastrous consequences. The overarching point to be made here is that change does not happen in a vacuum. We must never become so focused or obsessed with specific changes that we become oblivious to the larger picture.

Should we go ahead with change if we know it's the right thing to do? Shouldn't we ignore some old-fogy person or some outdated practice if they stand in the way of progress? This is the tricky part. Our motive may not be enough. The best motives in the world cannot remedy an ill-conceived plan. I have heard more than one pastor lament, "If I had it to do over, I would never have allowed this to be done." Good changes, right changes, and timely changes, even if they are extremely difficult, will flow better if we plan ahead for all the ramifications they cause. These same changes will fail miserably if we skip these preliminary steps.

As the Olympic hockey team found out, don't destroy a perfectly good chandelier.

Chapter 15
Read Writers and Right Readers

And these things write we unto you, that your joy may be full (I John 1:4).

Readers and writers have to work at their relationship. Since most readers aren't writers, they don't like to read about writing. Almost all writers, however, are readers. Readers read about subjects that interest them. Writers read articles on any subject, not just out of personal interest but because they want to know how the article was written.

There are exceptions, of course. Writers can entice readers to read almost anything if they create interesting, controversial, outrageous, or, at least, hilariously funny stuff. Thus, readers may read avidly about deoxyribonucleic acid, the history of Herodotus or Baroque music—all potentially boring subjects—if a writer can snare them with the cunning of his craft. Writers, on the other hand, may toss an article about an interesting subject if they find the writing insufferably poor. They

The View from the Back of the Pulpit

suspect a bad writer is probably an equally bad thinker or researcher. So even though a writer winces from carpal tunnel pain, is planning a vacation to Fiji, or is about to build a solar-heated log cabin, he would drop an article on these subjects like a worn-out cliché if the writer cannot write. ~~Strange, but true~~.

You, brave reader, couldn't care less about my tribulations with clichés, deadlines, mental blocks, or occasional bouts with irritable vowels. You have no idea why I chose a certain word over a score of possibilities, nor do you care. It does not make a cat's whisker's worth of difference to you that my word processor proves that I cranked out thirty revisions of the same article before emailing it to my editor. The words are on the paper, and you are oblivious to my struggle to put them there. You read for information or entertainment, period.

So are readers right in preferring substance to style? Or do writers who value style over substance get read more often? Certainly, a bad subject poorly written has no chance of getting read. Good writing on a bad subject is a waste of talent, whereas a good subject written poorly is tragic. A good subject written well represents the best of all choices. Substance, by itself, may be okay, but substance with style wins big.

Preachers are like writers. They cannot preach untruths and maintain their integrity at the same time. Yes, some do preach hermeneutically challenged sermons but, because they speak with splash and style, still gain a following. Those who preach the truth in a dull, colorless way may have their doctrine straight, but they preach to a pitifully narrow audience. The best choice remains the same with preaching as for writing: to preach the full truth with all the style and excellence a preacher has at his disposal. The same principle holds true for witnessing or any other venue for declaring the gospel.

Warren Wiersbe makes a good point when he says that churches are not in the *manufacturing* but the *distribution* business. We handle the greatest product ever produced. While the substance of the gospel may not be improved, the packaging can certainly be affected. Preachers must package and deliver truth to a desperate world with all the love, excitement, and excellence they can muster. Amens ought to be animated, not yawned. Good doctrine, good people, good church, and good preaching spell excitement!

The most valuable piece of advice on writing I have found is a principle pounded home by William Zinsser in his book *On Writing Well*. He strongly believes that there are no good writers—only good *re*-writers. Any writer who is not willing to redo his work will never be widely read, if he gets read at all. When I write, I always go back to read what I have written after several days. If it disappoints me, I revise it. (I've just passed revision number fifty-eight on this one, and there are more to come.) If it bores me, I trash it. When a writer can't get excited about his own subject, no one else will either. A read writer is a relentless re-writer.

Like a read writer, a *heard* preacher tears his sermons apart and puts them back together over and over again until they say what he wants them to say, with as

The View from the Back of the Pulpit

much power and succinctness as possible and with as much documentation and proof-texting as necessary. I wonder how many preachers would fall asleep listening to their own sermons if it were not so hard to sleep and talk at the same time? (Then again, I've heard of people talking in their sleep.) Every preacher ought to want his hearers' lives to be radically changed by the preached Word. High goals like this can only be achieved through excellence, and true excellence is born in the crucible of honing and perfecting one's craft. Poor preaching gets endured. Well-preached sermons get heard. Listeners may not know how you do it (114 revisions), but they will love the results.

Chapter 16
The Power to Destroy or the Power to Redeem

Whatsoever thou shalt bind on earth shall be bound in heaven: and whatsoever thou shalt loose on earth shall be loosed in heaven (Matthew 16:19).

Given half a chance, I'm more likely to complicate a simple subject than to simplify a complex one. Maybe that's why I have always tried to give the "binding and loosing" words of Jesus to Simon Peter a deep, unfathomable meaning. Even now, I can't shake some lingering suspicions that this is true, but I also believe something lies here that the church desperately needs today.

First, I concede that Jesus handed a decree to Peter that carried awesome authority. Peter exercised this authority when he told the crowd at Pentecost to repent, be baptized, and receive the Holy Ghost. It authorized him to extend the grace of God to the Samaritans in Acts chapter eight and to preach to the Gentiles in the tenth chapter. It quite possibly formed the basis for the church's authority to settle the quarrel

The View from the Back of the Pulpit

with the Judaizers and draft the four-part prohibition in Acts chapter fifteen.

While we may enthusiastically applaud these religious and racial breakthroughs, is it not possible that Peter, by the same authority, *could have refused to admit the Samaritans*? Could he have denied the household of Cornelius the chance to hear the gospel? Suddenly, we get clammy palms at the prospect of such authority. Some may dispute the logic of this contention, but certainly somebody, if not Peter, was clearly given the power to bind or loose. Come again? Did Jesus actually place in the hands of the church the power to forbid or to permit?

Peter, in fact, did not have *all* the keys. Jesus retained possession of the keys of hell, death, and the bottomless pit. But he did give to Peter and, in a larger sense, to the church the critical responsibility to open or close the kingdom door. Wherever the church evangelizes and to whomever it preaches the gospel, souls have a chance to be saved. At the same time, wherever the church refuses to go or from whomever the church withholds the message of salvation, the light will not shine. Romans 10:14-15 says,

> *How then shall they call on him in whom they have not believed? and how shall they believe in him of whom they have not heard? and how shall they hear without a preacher? And how shall they preach, except they be sent? as it is written, How beautiful are the feet of them that preach the gospel of peace, and bring glad tidings of good things!*

The Power to Destroy or the Power to Redeem

Except for the occasional Ethiopian eunuch who travels to Jerusalem on his own initiative, the gospel only goes where the church goes!

One simple question begs to be asked: Will you bind or loose? Will you preach the gospel of destruction or redemption? Are you driven to condemn the lost or to reconcile them to Christ? Your prevailing attitude will set the tone for church shrinkage or revivalistic growth.

Make no mistake about it, the truth can destroy. Piercing, pointed, indisputable facts straight out of the Scriptures can deliver a staggering blow. The Word can be a hammer, a sword, or a fire. If we choose, we can sculpt the gospel into a grotesque monster with fangs and claws and do it with proof texts and exegetical aplomb. The preacher who uses the truth to hurt may be right, but he is not smart. When truth is wielded as a weapon, the wounds it causes are not the fault of the truth but of the one who uses it. Truth yields itself to the form of the hand that grasps it.

The capacity to destroy does not ennoble the church. Jesus rebuked the disciples for enjoying their use of power over demons. He urged us to model the patient, waiting Father, the seeker of the lost coin, the compassionate shepherd who hazards his life for his sheep. When we berate, belittle, tongue-lash, and ridicule, we destroy. When we encourage, love, and comfort, we redeem. When we mock, rip, disrespect, and condemn, we destroy. When we understand, respect, praise, and honor, we redeem. When we denounce, rail, and call names, we destroy. When we preach the Word,

The View from the Back of the Pulpit

the Spirit, and the blood, we redeem.

The ministry of reconciliation defines our mission. We redeem by loving, not hating. We save by reaching, not repelling. We fulfill the great commission by indiscriminately sowing the gospel seed, not discriminating against hearers. Too many preachers commandeer the gospel truth for their own ego-advancing opportunities.

Jesus did not come into the world to condemn the world. Why, then, should we presume to do what He declined to do? Be a reconciler!

> *But all things are of God, who reconciled us to himself through Christ, and gave unto us the ministry of reconciliation; to wit, that God was in Christ reconciling the world unto himself, not reckoning unto them their trespasses, and having committed unto us the word of reconciliation* (II Corinthians 5:18-19, ASV).

You have the power to destroy or the power to redeem. How will you use your power?

Chapter 17
Expensive Convictions

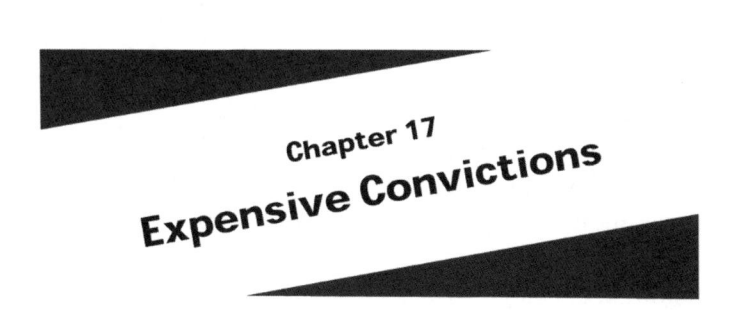

*I've got strong convictions 'bout the way that I live
I've got no concessions that I'm willing to give
Strong convictions that are worth living by
Strong convictions till the day I die.*
—Petra

Once lauded, strong convictions now face ridicule in society. In our alternate universe world, people who dare to hold strong convictions routinely get labeled stubborn, dogmatic, or hopelessly old-fashioned. They grow more and more distant from the world's lifestyles and belief systems. Their antagonists try to impose guilt feelings or even shame when they express ideas about what is going on in the world. Disdain for convictions pervades our culture.

Many years ago, attorney David Gibbs, then of the Christian Law Association, explained conviction as opposed to mere preference. Convictions, he said, will convince judges that a person is sincere, but preferences will be swept aside in favor of the state. Preferences

The View from the Back of the Pulpit

may vary according to time and circumstances, but convictions remain solid and unchangeable.

But beyond disdain, society now won't even tolerate men and women of conviction. Their anachronistic ideas elicit fierce protest in schools, courts, workplaces, and especially the media. They are told that they don't belong. As change streaks through our culture at warp speed, those who refuse to buckle pay dearly for their intransigence. The world reserves its understanding and compassion only for those who change. They hold in contempt those who do not or will not change.

The litany of things that were once opposed with strong convictions by the majority of people, but now are generally accepted, is long and growing. Abortion, unwed motherhood, cohabitation, homosexuality, same-sex adoptions, and euthanasia appear on a short list. Add to that public nudity, four-letter words, gross behavior, bizarre fashions, and sex education. These have all now become commonplace because convictions against them have withered under the heat of the opposition.

Have these issues triumphed because they are inherently right? Hardly. They have benefited from the unwillingness of people to hold to convictions and risk being branded as pigheaded or intolerant. Many have become conditioned to abandon their convictions simply because society views such beliefs as old-fashioned and today's majority rejects them. It's not what you believe but how strongly you believe it that draws the ire of the world around you.

Today, society brands convictions as a form of intolerance. Dr. Paul Kienel, past president of the Asso-

Expensive Convictions

ciation of Christian Schools International, writes about the new thinking in secular educational circles. He says that tolerance itself has come under scrutiny. Tolerance that says, "I disagree with you, but I still love you and will try to get along with you," is no longer acceptable. That is seen as negative tolerance. Political correctness now demands positive tolerance which says, "I agree that your viewpoint is right for you, and I support your desire to hold that view." One spokesperson for this opinion said, "The only thing we will not tolerate is intolerance."

Those who hold strong convictions based on biblical teachings are especially under the gun today. The societal ills mentioned earlier comprise only part of these convictions. Also included are theological positions, the doctrine of salvation, world and home missions, and biblical standards of dress and conduct. Those who cling to these positions suffer mounting pressure to lose their dogmatism. Again, the question is not the correctness of their views, but the rigidity with which they hold them. Those who preach against or publicly criticize the homosexual lifestyle and same-sex marriage may soon be charged with a criminal act. Those who teach and enforce a biblical standard of dress and behavior may soon be found guilty of abuse. Bible believers may be

> **It's not only what you believe but how strongly you believe it that draws the ire of the world around you.**

The View from the Back of the Pulpit

told either to back off or go to jail. As preposterous as this seems, the trends point in that direction.

Jesus said, "And ye shall be hated of all men for my name's sake: but he that shall endure unto the end, the same shall be saved" (Mark 13:13). No figure in history more aptly illustrates the willingness to stand for a strongly held conviction than Jesus. He bowed to no pressure, whether political, emotional, physical, or psychological. Neither Herod nor Pilate, the Pharisees nor the Roman soldiers fazed Him. Judas's betrayal, Peter's defection, and the disciples' attempts to stop Him from going to the cross did not change His mind. Discomfort, inconvenience, loneliness, or fear did not mitigate His commitment to His convictions.

Since its beginnings, the United Pentecostal Church, International, has stood amazingly strong against the tide of contrary opinion. The price we pay to maintain this stand will probably not decrease. As property taxes assessed against homeowners inevitably rise, so also those who continue to reside at the same biblical and moral positions where they have always lived should expect the rent to go up. Convictions never go on sale.

The only way we can continue to afford expensive convictions is to tap into the mother lode of grace and truth. God gives grace, power, and boundless strength to those who commit themselves totally to Him. When convictions become preferences, when standards become optional, when we remodel the straight and narrow way into a more "user-friendly" broad way, when "thus saith the Lord" changes to "thus saith the world," we will end up evicted and out on the street.

Expensive Convictions

How long has it been since you read apostle Peter's words? "For you have spent enough time in the past doing what pagans choose to do—living in debauchery, lust, drunkenness, orgies, carousing and detestable idolatry. They think it strange that you do not plunge with them into the same flood of dissipation, and they heap abuse on you" (I Peter 4:3-4, NIV). Again, Peter wrote,

> *Dear friends, do not be surprised at the painful trial you are suffering, as though something strange were happening to you. But rejoice that you participate in the sufferings of Christ, so that you may be overjoyed when his glory is revealed. If you are insulted because of the name of Christ, you are blessed, for the Spirit of glory and of God rests on you. If you suffer, it should not be as a murderer or thief or any other kind of criminal, or even as a meddler. However, if you suffer as a Christian, do not be ashamed, but praise God that you bear that name* (I Peter 4:12-16, NIV).

The suffering Peter referred to may not have been physical only, but also emotional and psychological.

The neighborhood of believers has seen a major transition. Those who stick with strong convictions now find themselves in a high-rent district. But convictions that rest firmly upon the foundation of God's Word cannot move. When the pressure to change ratchets up, let it serve only to reinforce our commitment. Suffering must not dislodge us. If we suffer for the name of Jesus, let it not be our veil of shame but our badge of honor.

Chapter 18
When Leaders Sin

I have sinned against the LORD (II Samuel 12:13).

Many readers of this book will probably skip this chapter. I understand. Who wants to read about sin? Negative approaches to leadership never inspire us—certainly not me—to achieve greater goals. If anyone has a strong bias toward the positive, I do. Yet there are times when I find myself trying to figure out why leaders fail or why their strategies consistently blow up in their faces. It appears that they are doing everything right, yet they can never pull off the successes they desire. The reasons they cite for their failures seem unlikely or downright weird. When nothing makes sense, I begin to suspect that sin is the underlying problem. My suspicions are not always right, but they have been confirmed often enough to warrant a thorough examination of the subject.

The exposure of a spiritual leader's sin goes far beyond the typical embarrassment and shame that non-leaders suffer. The leader risks his livelihood, position, career, and very identity. This gives him an enormous incentive to hide his sin. At the same time, no other individual's sin carries with it a greater reason for punishment, primarily because the leader represents moral and ethical purity to his followers. The charge of hypocrisy dogs every mistake a leader makes.

When leaders' sins are exposed, the repercussions reach seismic proportions. Stories of hugely popular televangelists who fell from their pinnacles of success still circulate in the culture. Church organizations or denominations whose leaders have sinned bear nationwide scars from the scandals. Even in local communities or individual churches, failed leaders damage the faith and confidence of hundreds of people.

What happens when a leader sins?

Sin insults God. Joseph understood this principle long before Moses descended from Mt. Sinai with the Ten Commandments. "How then can I do this great wickedness, and sin against God?" (Genesis 39:9). The first thing a spiritual leader must realize is that his sin dramatically affects his relationship with God. This seems obvious enough, but I am totally flummoxed at the way some leaders will negotiate, justify, equivocate, and otherwise try to get around this ghastly elephant in their living rooms. One cannot force-feed God that which God abhors.

Sin entraps. Moses predicted this unforeseen result of sin in Exodus 23:33. "They shall not dwell in thy land, lest they make thee sin against me: for if thou serve their gods, it will surely be a snare unto thee." Like the ancient Chinese finger trap, one may easily enter into the act of sin but soon find that it is impossible to back out of it. One minister found out that the sweet, little, clingy teenager who only needed the comfort of a strong male figure in her life turned into a vicious, manipulative hustler once she had him in her clutches.

As every coin has an obverse and reverse, every act of sin has two sides: Commit the sin; cover the sin. The instant a sin is committed, the flip side comes into play. Moreover, sin comes with consequences included. No one has to add them or order them separately.

Sin affects the people you lead. Exodus 32:21, "And Moses said unto Aaron, What did this people unto thee, that thou hast brought so great a sin upon them?" Whatever character flaws or unrepented transgressions lodged in the heart of Aaron, they did not exist in a vacuum. Aware of it or not, his sins impacted Israel. Every leader's proffered ideas find formulation within the confines of his heart. The tarnished heart, the misguided spirit, and the corrupted soul of the leader shape the message that proceeds from his mouth into destructive plans for his followers. Jesus said, "But those things which proceed out of the mouth come forth from the heart; and they defile the man" (Matthew 15:18).

Some leaders mistakenly believe that their personal, private life has no bearing on their ability to lead. But the leader who sins leads his people in a different way than he should. He will deliver his message with a different tone, a different emphasis, and a noticeable lack of conviction. The substance of his message will be evasive and noncommittal in doctrinal content. He will have less heart for enforcement of church polity than his people deserve.

Sin cannot go unpunished. "And if a man have committed a sin worthy of death, and he be to be put to death, and thou hang him on a tree" (Deuteronomy 21:22). When we sweep sin under the rug, when we treat it differently from person to person, or when we simply let it go unpunished, the sinning person gets a false view of God's justice. A leader cannot afford to be dismissive, tolerant, or defensive of sin. Without consequences, sin loses its dread. A diminished view of sin either results from or leads to a diminished view of Calvary. Ambivalence toward sin casts doubt on the efficacious blood of Jesus.

Sin opens the door to other sins. "For rebellion is as the sin of witchcraft, and stubbornness is as iniquity and idolatry. Because thou hast rejected the word of the LORD, he hath also rejected thee from being king" (I Samuel 15:23). How can rebellion possibly be related to witchcraft? How could iniquity ever share common ground with stubbornness and idolatry? Because all branches of sin grow from the same trunk. That's why John the Baptist said, "And now also the axe is laid unto the root of the trees" (Matthew 3:10). The root of offense gives rise to many sinful branches. Saul did not conquer his initial disobedience; therefore, he experienced a chain reaction of repeated sin and tragedy in his life. King David's lust led to adultery; his adultery led to deceit; his deceit led to murder. On and on it goes. Once the essence of sin gains entrance into one's life, it brings with it the seeds of further transgressions. James said, "For where envying and strife is, there is confusion and every evil work" (James 3:16).

Sin obeys the law of precedent. When someone commits one sin, the next one seems much easier. The first sin excuses the next. Many would not think of committing sin "D"—that is, until they first committed "A," then "B," then "C." The leader enjoys no exemption from the law of sin.

Sin gives occasion for God's enemies to rejoice. "Howbeit, because by this deed thou hast given great occasion to the enemies of the LORD to blaspheme, the child also that is born unto thee shall surely die" (II Samuel 12:14). These bitter words came from Nathan, the prophet, when he castigated David for the sins of adultery and murder. David's iniquity brought great reproach to Israel. Sin always seems worse when committed by the leader because he represents all his followers. When leaders sin, they damage the credibility of everyone in the camp.

Sin causes others to sin. "And he did evil in the sight of the LORD, and walked in the way of Jeroboam, and in his sin wherewith he made Israel to sin" (I Kings 15:34). Jeroboam may have denied this charge, but Israel's sin was laid at his feet. Why? Authority figures possess inherent culpability. We shame sinful parents for misleading their children; we become outraged at teachers who incite their students to sin; we condemn scout leaders who corrupt their young followers. Leaders have influence; in fact, it is widely accepted that leadership *is* influence. The leader who sins, therefore, causes his followers to sin by proxy. He cannot feign innocence for the sins of his followers and cite their free moral agency to make their own decisions.

Sin causes restlessness to the soul. "There is no soundness in my flesh because of thine anger; neither is there any rest in my bones because of my sin" (Psalm 38:3). Confidence constitutes one of leadership's most vital traits and reproduces itself in the lives of followers. Sin has a deleterious effect on the inner man, the subconscious soul that determines a person's peace and integrity. It causes self-doubt, loss of conviction, and timidity of faith. Whether he knows it or not, the leader who sins hollows out the core of his leadership ability.

Sin dogs the conscience. "For I acknowledge my transgressions: and my sin is ever before me" (Psalm 51:3). After his wanton indulgence with Bathsheba, David discovered the debilitating nature of sin. A guilty conscience clouds judgment and turns away from pure truth. No leader can afford to live in sin and remain engaged in leadership. Leadership demands too much selfless sacrifice to allow the distraction of a troubled conscience. Fallen leaders lose their effectiveness from wallowing in personal anguish and self-absorption.

Sin turns prayer into sin. Psalm 109:7, "When he shall be judged, let him be condemned: and let his prayer become sin." Sin impairs judgment to the extent that people actually ask God to bless their sinning ways. Balaam tried this tactic, but God would not let him succeed.

They have gone off the road and become lost like Balaam, the son of Beor, who fell in love with the money he could make by doing wrong; but Balaam was stopped from his mad course when his donkey spoke to him with a human voice, scolding and rebuking him (II Peter 2:15-16, TLB).

When leaders who find themselves entrapped in wrongdoing pray to extend or preserve their sin, they cause their very prayers to become sin.

Sin is mocked only by fools. "Fools make a mock at sin: but among the righteous there is favour" (Proverbs 14:9). Any spiritual leader who mocks sin cannot be serious or sincere. His leadership will be a sham. Serious and sincere followers will eventually abandon him.

Sin seeks out refuge in godless counsel. "Woe to the rebellious children, saith the LORD, that take counsel, but not of me; and that cover with a covering, but not of my spirit, that they may add sin to sin" (Isaiah 30:1). When the leader knows that his sin is the problem but is not willing to confess it, he often seeks counsel from unbelievers or reprobates in an attempt to change the consequences. Such practices add sin to sin.

Sin separates. "Behold, the LORD'S hand is not shortened, that it cannot save; neither his ear heavy, that it cannot hear: but your iniquities have separated between you and your God, and your sins have hid his face from you, that he will not hear" (Isaiah 59:1-2). The leader cannot get direction from God for his mission because his sin acts as a wall of separation between God and himself. Regardless of his scholarship, charismatic personality, or administrative skills, his broken connection with God renders him ineffective.

Sin becomes your master. "Jesus answered them, Verily, verily, I say unto you, Whosoever committeth sin is the servant of sin" (John 8:34). This scriptural truth becomes exponentially dangerous in leadership. The righteous leader functions as God's spokesperson, the giver of the clear and certain sound, the one with whom God entrusts the welfare of His flock. Such a sacred duty demands a free and pure exchange of thought between the shepherd and the Lord. When sin enters a leader's life, however, God no longer dictates the direction and quality of his leadership. Sin takes over that function. The sinning leader becomes intent on that which protects his sin and avoids that which threatens to expose his sin. Instead of his private study serving as a quest for God, it turns into a place of scheming for ways to get around God. Heretical doctrine and reprobation follow hard on the heels of sinning leaders.

Sin against knowledge offends the law of God. "Therefore by the deeds of the law there shall no flesh be justified in his sight: for by the law is the knowledge of sin" (Romans 3:20). Harboring sin in his heart causes the leader to subvert the very law he is called to teach or to practice. This cannot continue for long because the Word of God is alive and it discerns the soul and spirit of a man. The spiritual leader who deliberately mishandles the Word of God plays with fire.

Sin wounds weak consciences. "But when ye sin so against the brethren, and wound their weak conscience, ye sin against Christ" (I Corinthians 8:12). Regardless of his attempts to be subtle, the leader who sins bruises the souls in his charge. Too weak to overcome his wrong or too ignorant to protect themselves against it, his followers stray from the beaten path. The transgressor makes merchandise of men's souls.

Sin disqualifies the leader from rebuking sin. "Them that sin rebuke before all, that others also may fear" (I Timothy 5:20). The duty to rebuke sin in others becomes difficult or impossible to do for the leader who has sin in his own life. Thus, he is prevented from caring for the flock of God.

Sin hardens. "But exhort one another daily, while it is called To day; lest any of you be hardened through the deceitfulness of sin" (Hebrews 3:13). The hardening process takes years, but, eventually, it destroys all sensitivity to the Spirit of God. The hardened leader who cannot follow Christ cannot lead people to Christ. He gradually grows numb to warning signals in church culture and in individual lives; thus, he says yes when he should say no, he opens gates that should remain closed, and he grants favor when he should establish prohibition.

Sin entangles. "Wherefore seeing we also are compassed about with so great a cloud of witnesses, let us lay aside every weight, and the sin which doth so easily beset us, and let us run with patience the race that is set before us" (Hebrews 12:1). *Beset* means "to entangle." Leaders who sin spin convoluted webs to invent alternative solutions to sin and alternative philosophies to truth. Confusion, contradiction, and inconsistency permeate their position and message. That which was once starkly clear in their minds slips into shadowy indistinctness. They champion causes they were once against; they rail against those things they once affirmed. They arrive at new positions daily, and each change forces a shift in their reasoning to substantiate their latest opinion. Eventually, they resign themselves to acting out the charade in an effort to survive until retirement.

Sin causes death. "Then when lust hath conceived, it bringeth forth sin: and sin, when it is finished, bringeth forth death" (James 1:15). The leader who sins sounds the death knell to his own leadership and ministry. If he truly believes the Bible that he preaches, it cannot be otherwise. If he preaches something different, he cannot believe the Bible. Either way, his anointing vanishes and his ministry collapses.

What is the solution for the leader who sins?

Accountability. The leader who sins needs to submit to his spiritual authority. God has so ordered the nature of man that he cannot exist in a vacuum, unanswerable and unassailable. The fallen leader must voluntarily place himself in a vulnerable position and become accountable.

Assessment of the context. Many factors govern the disposition of the problem. The leader may not need to be totally defrocked. He may need a time of silence; he may need to confess publicly; he may need a demotion or a restriction; he may need to offer restitution, and so on. His spiritual authorities need to determine the penalties and repercussions.

Application of David's repentance. Whatever may be necessary to amend damage to his followers, the sinning leader's personal restoration must involve thorough repentance in the fashion of David's penitential psalm.

David's steps to restoration: Psalm 51:1-13.

Appeal to mercy. Verse 1, "Have mercy upon me, O God, according to thy lovingkindness: according unto the multitude of thy tender mercies blot out my transgressions." No equivocation here. David's forthright appeal to God's mercy underscored his comprehension of God. The God of absolute truth brooks no insincerity; how could He do so without corrupting His purity? David knew he could not manipulate God into a compromising position. Like David, the sinning leader must abase himself before he can expect favor with God. He must not hide behind his past accomplishments, the respect he thinks he deserves, his latent talent, or his continued ability to lead. All that is negated by the sin he committed.

Acknowledgment of sin. Verse 3, "For I acknowledge my transgressions: and my sin is ever before me." For clarity, we move to verse three, in which David acknowledged his transgression. David did not deny, recharacterize, or minimize his sin. He did not criticize Nathan for confronting him; he did not formulate elaborate excuses for his actions; he did not blame Bathsheba for seducing him; he did not curse Uriah for his stupidity; he did not cast aspersions on God for creating him "that way." He simply, bluntly admitted his sin.

Washing and cleansing. Verse 2, "Wash me throughly from mine iniquity, and cleanse me from my sin." Despite their similarity, washing and cleansing mean two different things. Washing is the action that cleanses, but cleansing refers to the result. We wash in order to achieve cleansing. David knew he needed to take action to eradicate his sin—repentance, confession, restitution—but the results could not be superficial or tokenism. The leader cannot make grandiose, public charades that he has taken care of his wrongdoing but resist real change. He must experience a true metamorphosis in both status and state of his soul, mind, and spirit.

Understanding of grievance. Verse 4, "Against thee, thee only, have I sinned, and done this evil in thy sight: that thou mightest be justified when thou speakest, and be clear when thou judgest." David demonstrated penetrating insight in this statement. He did not cast his sin as a mere faux pas against people; he correctly realized that his sin ultimately offended God alone. It was clear to David that his sin was God's business. A spiritual leader cannot continue to operate under the guise of "paying off" the victim or of clandestinely taking care of an inconvenient problem that his sin caused with an associate and assume that his relationship with God remains untouched. Such minimal lateral actions fall short of true justice and they only set the offender up for a repeat offense. David was not arraigned in the lower courts of human behavior but in the Supreme Court of heaven where the almighty God sits on the bench.

Understanding of God's true purpose. Verse 6, "Behold, thou desirest truth in the inward parts: and in the hidden part thou shalt make me to know wisdom."

Finally, David fully embraced the overarching purpose of God: truth in the inward parts. God is not about diplo-speak, pretense, or affected displays of repentance. He doesn't traffic in looking good or seeming to be right. God is about truth at the core of our being. Repentance that does not take us all the way to nuclear truth always fails. We cannot marginalize God's righteousness. We cannot engage Him in a chess match as though we were capable of outmaneuvering Him. Leaders whose lives do not exemplify core truth will corrupt their followers.

Purging process. Verse 7, "Purge me with hyssop, and I shall be clean: wash me, and I shall be whiter than snow." Purging requires the bristles of a scrub brush, the stinging acid of cleansing agents, the razored edge of the surgeon's scalpel, or perhaps even the ripping teeth of a saw to amputate a limb. Contamination must not be permitted to hide in cracks and corners or dive under layers of tissue to escape notice. David not only submitted to the rigors of the purging process, but he *invited* it. The difference is in the attitude. A leader must not endure the mortification of exposure and restitution with an air of annoyance as though he were above it all. He must actively engage the process. It represents more than the penalty for his sin; it is the only path to full restoration. Refusing to accept total purging testifies to incomplete repentance.

Spiritual goal setting. Verse 8, "Make me to hear joy and gladness; that the bones which thou hast broken may rejoice." The emotions of hurt, shame, and embarrassment accompany the outing of sin. Those caught up in the ordeal must resist the urge to wallow in negativity and lick their wounds. Refocusing on positive spiritual goals remains the only viable option. Joy, gladness, and rejoicing flow from the born-again soul. David's blighted soul had not had cause to rejoice for months, yet he understood that the well could spring up again. The sweet psalmist could once again sing a new song; music could again be caressed from the harp that guilt had flung into a corner. David's sin was human, but his restoration divine.

New creation. Verse 10, "Create in me a clean heart, O God; and renew a right spirit within me." Two stark truths stand out here. First, the leader who sins must recognize that his problem is deep-seated, calling for the creation of a purity he never before possessed. He cannot point to all his positives as though they somehow make up for his corrupt deeds. Thinking that *he* could not be that monster who sinned, only perpetuates his error. He needs a clean heart and a right spirit. Second, he has to admit that he is incapable of remaking himself. Few things are tougher for a self-assured, independent man known for his leadership abilities than to meekly ask for help. He needs more than time, space, and understanding. He must undergo a fundamental shift in his self-image.

Restoration. Verse 12, "Restore unto me the joy of thy salvation; and uphold me with thy free spirit." Restoration involves the repaired relationship between a forgiven sinner and two other entities: his God and his fellow man. When he mends these relationships, joy and freedom burst forth as a result. David longed for a return to innocence when he could feel the same joy he felt as a shepherd boy tending his father's sheep. But a restored joy does not have innocence to support it. It has to be upheld with the Spirit of God.

Resumption of ministry. Verse 13, "Then will I teach transgressors thy ways; and sinners shall be converted unto thee." Ministry can only be resumed at the end of a long, sometimes arduous process. Notice that David did not put the burden of proof on God by saying, "Then you must let me teach again." God has nothing to prove. David knew that restoration remained impossible without a thorough application of the divine remedy. He fully understood that his effectiveness as a teacher rested on completing the process. Anything less would be presumptuous and cheap. The leader who sins has no right to be angry with people who have a hard time accepting his renewal. He must understand their skepticism and work to overcome it.

The leader who sins must come to terms with certain irreversible facts: he will be forever changed. Some will never accept him; some will accept him but always with a tinge of mistrust; he will live with a fence around a piece of his personal history. The often overlooked factor of the prodigal son who returned is that he did not pick up where he left off. He had to rebuild his inheritance starting at ground zero. So also is the present and future of the restored leader. A fulfilling life will not unfold without a complete appreciation of his wrongdoing and a total commitment to change.

Chapter 19
Issues in Retirement for Pastors

Is Retirement for a Minister in the Will of God?

Not long ago, many ministers scorned the idea of retirement. They felt that a preacher who retired betrayed the call of God in his life. Others believed the rapture of the church was so imminent that there was no need to prepare for retirement. Indeed, a minister who thought too far ahead about his own security and welfare was deemed carnal.

A study of Scripture, however, demonstrates that 1) age brings about a diminished physical stamina; 2) age changes a man's role in life; 3) there are age limitations placed upon the years that a priest could actively serve; and 4) the leadership spans of many notable leaders in Scripture followed a predictable pattern of longevity.

Age brings about a diminished physical stamina. We understand this as a fact of life, but what does the Scripture say?

The View from the Back of the Pulpit

Judah is a lion's whelp: from the prey, my son, thou art gone up: he stooped down, he couched as a lion, and as an old lion; who shall rouse him up? (Genesis 49:9).

I am this day fourscore years old: and can I discern between good and evil? can thy servant taste what I eat or what I drink? can I hear any more the voice of singing men and singing women? wherefore then should thy servant be yet a burden unto my lord the king? (II Samuel 19:35).

Age changes a person's role in life. An individual's value as a counselor becomes much greater than his or her ability to do physical work.

Thou shalt rise up before the hoary head, and honour the face of the old man, and fear thy God: I am the LORD (Leviticus 19:32).

And king Rehoboam consulted with the old men, that stood before Solomon his father while he yet lived, and said, How do ye advise that I may answer this people? (I Kings 12:6).

The Old Testament Scriptures indicate that limitations were placed upon the active service of all priests, and of leaders in general.

And thy estimation shall be of the male from twenty years old even unto sixty years old, even thy estima-

tion shall be fifty shekels of silver, after the shekel of the sanctuary (Leviticus 27:3).

From thirty years old and upward even until fifty years old, all that enter into the host, to do the work in the tabernacle of the congregation (Numbers 4:3).

David was thirty years old when he began to reign, and he reigned forty years (II Samuel 5:4).

In addition to scriptural examples of aging preachers, I personally feel that a minister—especially a pastor—enters a stage of his life in which he begins to lose influence over the youthful segment of his congregation. After he turns fifty, those twenty years younger or more cease viewing him as a role model. They may love him, they may respect him, but they no longer want to be like him. His vocabulary, style, illustrations, clothing—nearly everything about him becomes dated. It's not that they want him to have an extreme makeover and pretend he's a young evangelist again. That would be phony. They want either a younger pastor or at least someone waiting in the wings who will have a relevant, in-touch ministry. They want the security of a viable future. A younger man represents the future.

What Issues Does a Retiring Minister Face?

Age means a diminished ability to continue in life's work. Do not ignore the prospect of retirement.

The View from the Back of the Pulpit

Retirement causes so many profound changes in a minister's life that the very thought can be frightening. It paralyzes many into inaction and even denial. Yet the changes retirement brings are both irreversible and inevitable. The most basic issues to be considered are: 1) financial security; 2) selection of a successor; 3) transitional process; and 4) life after retirement.

Procrastination is deadly. We will look at each of these issues, but the operative word here is *face*. Reality is a stubborn thing. It will not go away. The man who refuses to confront the matter only engages in futile self-deception. Procrastination is seldom a virtue, but in this regard, it looks more like a flagrant vice.

The responsible minister must ask himself three questions: 1) What will happen to my church? 2) What will happen to my spouse? 3) Will I become a burden to others? Responsibility dictates action. In our active years, we do not expect anyone else to buy our groceries or pay our bills. Neither should we expect anyone to shoulder our responsibilities in our retirement years.

Financial Security

Start now. Regardless of your age, you must begin now to prepare. If you are ignorant of money matters, you may obtain good financial advice from professional sources. Anyone who can shop for a car or a house is able to shop for financial services as well. At least three areas need to be explored in terms of personal finance: 1) Disciplined savings, 2) IRA or Keogh plans, 3) The principle of compounding interest. Find out the facts about all of these things.

Warning: The later you start, the greater amounts you must save. This comes as a great shock to ministers who waited until late in life to think about retirement. Some retirees have fallen from a comfortable, middle-class income into abject poverty in less than a year. While that may be extreme, certainly no one can continue to live at his current standard with an income that is cut in half. You would be better off to voluntarily downsize while you are preparing for retirement than to be forced to do it later. Bite the bullet now.

Is Social Security enough? In a word, no. The best Social Security can do is keep you off welfare. If you are counting on it to provide the bulk of your retirement income, you must prepare yourself for a huge letdown —no travel, no new cars, few new clothes, no vacations, no remodeling or redecorating, no gift-giving, no frills. You may be able to buy food and gasoline, pay your insurance and utilities, and purchase a few of the other necessities of life. After that, you will run out of money.

How much can the church contribute? This question lies at the heart of many ministerial retirement decisions. Most members and pastors alike believe that the congregation should do everything possible to provide a pension, if the church can afford it. Greater consideration should be given to a founding pastor or a pastor who has invested the bulk of his career into a church. Some churches pay into a pension fund set up for their pastor. Obviously, the viability of this plan depends upon how much is set aside in each period and how soon the program was started prior to retirement. Some churches give the pastor a lump sum upon retirement, even if they have to mortgage the church building or property to do it. Others arrange for the retiring pastor to receive a percentage of the tithing income. Still others give a pastor a set amount each week or month. The best plan for a given church depends upon its financial strength.

The role of the church in retirement hinges upon the leadership of the retiring pastor. If he initiates the action, the church will probably comply cheerfully. Many pastors hesitate to do this because they don't want to seem selfish or they can't justify paying for a retirement package when the church has trouble paying the electric bill. As a result, aging pastors have no retirement plans, and their churches do not realize it. When they find out, members feel terrible that they did not think about this situation years before when they could have done something about it. This situation causes many pastors to stay active despite poor health or diminished ability.

Is a contract necessary? Having a written contract is much better than having a mere verbal commitment. In our litigious society, properly prepared documents have become the expected way of doing business. Too many things can change between the onset of retirement and even a year afterwards. Most of the time, a resolution setting forth the terms of the retirement package and passed in a duly called business meeting of the church is the minimum requirement. It should specify how much, when, by whom the payments will be made,

Issues in Retirement for Pastors

and all other pertinent items. Make sure it clearly states whether or not the terms can be changed and how the changes can take place. Also, if the flow of payments are interrupted, the retiring pastor needs a proper channel to notify the church. Some believe that trust and integrity make such a contract unnecessary. Too many horror stories through the years suggest otherwise.

Keep in mind, however, that contracts may not always be honored. When subsequent changes occur in church leadership, an incoming pastor may not feel obligated to honor a document that he had no part in creating. He may also simply declare that the church can no longer afford the terms. If the majority of the congregation approves of his action, little can be done about it. Still, the likelihood that a retirement commitment will be honored increases with the existence of a written contract. It may not be foolproof, but it is better than nothing.

What if retirement seems financially impossible? At the risk of redundancy, let's summarize. 1) It will never get any easier. 2) Explore all the financial possibilities. 3) Ignoring it will not make the problem go away. 4) Aging pastors may have a shrinking financial base. Either a pastor will take care of these needs the best way he can at his own terms, or others will take care of them at their terms.

Selecting a Successor

Who will be the next pastor? A well-known leadership maxim holds that no one succeeds without a successor. Blessed indeed is the church whose pastor has provided for their future by bringing in an heir apparent. A move such as this requires that a pastor admits his diminished abilities and be willing to share his power and place the continuity of secure leadership above his personal position. These are noble qualities. Yet, in addition to the importance of such a choice, some practical issues need to be examined.

Can you afford to pay an assistant? Though other aspects of hiring an assistant are more important than money, affordability usually comes up first. Whatever you can pay, be up front about it. Set a salary; list other benefits such as housing, reimbursement for expenses, perquisites such as health insurance, conference expenses, and any other remuneration. Hard figures are easiest to work with because they help a new minister to know exactly where he stands. If you cannot be that specific about an assistant's income, try to give him a minimum figure. This will place the decision to accept the offer in his hands. If you plan on giving him a percentage of the tithing, he needs to be privy to the tithing totals. Openness produces trust.

Should you ask an assistant to work a secular job? If this is the only way you can get an assistant, it doesn't hurt to ask. Many ministers just getting started in the ministry may jump at the chance. You should understand, however, that there are some drawbacks to this arrangement. First, a job that pays a decent wage will probably demand time from the employee. You may end up without much of an assistant anyway. Also, most experienced ministers or those who are now full-time will probably not be interested in going back to secular work. Those who agree to do it are most likely looking at a short-term stint or may have shifted their focus away from the ministry as a career choice and see an assistant pastor's job as sideline work.

What are the expectations of an assistant? If a prospective assistant is one you would seriously consider as your replacement, factors other than remuneration enter into the offer. The most important factor involves his expectations. Several primary concerns are on his mind about the position. Here are some common expectations: 1) To assist and that's all. This minister has no desire to become a pastor. 2) To be the associate pastor with some authority. 3) A vague idea that he may someday become pastor. 4) A clear understanding that he will be pastor. A man who is considering the offer may accept less pay if he knows that he may become the pastor. The key to this arrangement must be good communication. Many pastors have lost good assistants because they failed to communicate with them about the future.

How do you know if you are being vague? The relationship between pastors and their assistants often declines because of communication problems. "But I thought you knew, . . ." "You should have known, . . ." "Couldn't you tell. . . ?" are all statements made by pastors who didn't realize the importance of good communication. Assistant pastors are not mind readers. If you don't tell them, they won't know. For either of you to assume something is to invite disappointment, if not disaster. If you are making the following statements, you are being too vague: 1) "If something happens to me . . ." *Like what? Retirement, sickness, death?* 2) "You never know what the future holds. . . ." *Got any ideas?* 3) "Just be faithful, and there will be a place for you." *For example?* 4) "I have plans. . . ." *Can you share them?*

Does a relative work out? Relatives such as sons, sons-in-law, etc. should be seen as a viable choice only if all other aspects of an assistant are acceptable. It certainly should not be the primary reason for selecting an assistant. If the pastor ever has to ask such an assistant to leave, family problems are almost certain to erupt. On the other hand, if the person demonstrates capable leadership, his family relationship may strengthen his position.

From the church's perspective, to be forced to accept leadership from someone whose only credentials is that he is a relative of the pastor is a bitter pill to swallow. Eventually, serious problems will result. Often, the church feels that they must go along with the new man because rejecting him will hurt the retiring pastor. The wise pastor will keep his eyes and ears open to monitor the response of the congregation during a probationary time.

Finally, a relative of the pastor should establish his ministry in places other than the local church. By doing so, he will greatly add to his credibility among the people. It is not good for a church to perceive that everything was handed to their leader on a "silver platter." Neither is it good for a man to assume a place of high authority without going through some intermediate steps to earn his status. In rare cases it may work, but most of the time a person who is given a position without paying his due takes his good fortune for granted.

What about a resume? More and more churches now request a resume from a prospective pastor. It is a brief, concise way of getting a lot of pertinent information which will help a congregation make a decision. If you do not know the man you are considering for an assistant, it may be helpful to ask him to send his resume. He should understand that you will check up on the references. As you study the resume, make sure you clarify any gaps in the chronological record.

Should you select a minister who is a member of the church? If he qualifies, yes. You should understand, however, that some people may not receive him because he is perceived as a peer. Remember, a prophet is not without honor except in his own house. On the other hand, there are some men who are such outstanding saints that they already have much respect among the people. This arrangement will vary from man to man and church to church.

Probationary Period

If retirement is not immediate or certain. Regardless of how well you admire or are impressed by someone at a distance, working with him up close usually presents a different picture. While you are adjusting to the idea of retirement, having an assistant come in will help you get a better understanding of the issues at stake. You need to know as much as possible about the person to whom you may turn the church. He needs to know you and the church. Love at first sight can fade just as swiftly. If you make a definite commitment prematurely, headache and heartache will follow.

Six-month to one-year probationary period. Before your retirement date and the installation of the new pastor, make sure you provide ample time to get acquainted with him. The length of time may be determined by the distance he has to move to relocate, whether or not he has to give up a present job or position, and how well you already know him. You certainly should not ask a man to move across the country at a great expense or to sacrifice a good job for you and then dismiss him in a few weeks. If you do find it necessary to end the relationship, compensate him fairly for his trouble.

Keep an open ear to the people during the probationary time. Your saints will let you know how they feel. Listen for comments—not just about his preaching—but teaching, conversation, interaction with people, attitudes, and other bits of information that indicate his acceptance. Also, there are certain things to watch for. Here are a few: 1) Character, 2) Willingness to work with you, 3) Undue interest in money issues, 4) Overstepping authority. Problems in these areas will probably grow larger over time.

Develop a written contract to avoid any misunderstanding. Just as your retirement agreement with the church should be in writing, so should your arrangement with an incoming assistant. The contract should primarily concern his job as an assistant before he becomes the pastor since it is this time period in which he will still be under your authority. It should specify a length of time before he becomes pastor, the qualifications that he needs to demonstrate in order to be elected, his compensation as an assistant, his job description, and any other necessary provisions.

You must make a definite commitment to change. The probationary period is for you as well as the new man. Sometimes pastors get "cold feet" with regard to their retirement. They may approve of the assistant but find that they are more reluctant than they previously thought to give it all up. There are also situations where the church responded to the new man and revival broke out. This made the retiring pastor feel differently about leaving. Use the time to clarify your own feelings to yourself. You must have a peace about your move. At the same time, remember that time is not on your side. Sooner or later, a decision will be necessary.

After Retirement

Should you move away? This point has so many variables that it is difficult to determine what to do. Some pastors want stay because: lack of money to move, poor health, close relatives in the church, the new pastor wants them to stay. Some leave because: climate, relatives who live elsewhere, poor relationship with the congregation, entering another phase of ministry.

What if you move? If you decide to move, either sever all ties with the church or channel all communication through the new pastor. Incidental contacts with people and talking about unimportant things will probably not cause difficulties, but you should not initiate a conversation to talk about church matters or any member's personal life without the pastor's knowledge. Besides being unethical, it makes it harder and prolongs the process for a smooth transition between pastors to take place.

What if you stay? If you stay, accept the fact that the new pastor will have a different style and focus to his ministry. Guard your feelings. Whenever you feel that the things you used to emphasize are not as important to him, back off and let him have his own ministry. Do not discuss pastoral related problems with the people. Give him as much cooperation as you desired from people when you were the pastor. Be a good saint.

What should you do with your time? Assuming that your health is good and that you have adequate finances, you probably will stay busy for the first year doing the things you always wanted to do. It is the second year and after that poses a problem. Accept some new challenges, get involved in some ventures that have always interested you, and make your retirement years count for something eternal. The possibilities are so numerous that I will not attempt to list them. One thing is sure: you need to plan your retirement and have an agenda to follow. Do anything except one—do not try to pastor the church you just left! If there is a rule of thumb about retirement, it is this: Retirement ought to keep you looking forward—not backward.

In summary, take care of your financial security, select a successor, watch the transition closely, and

Issues in Retirement for Pastors

know what you're going to do after retirement. If you do these things, you will multiply the blessings and minimize the difficulties of this time in your life.

Other books by J. Mark Jordan:

Living and Leading in Ministry
Living and Leading in Ministry audio CD

**To order from
Pentecostal Publishing House:**

8855 Dunn Road
Hazelwood, MO 63042-2299

Telephone: 314-837-7304, ext. 7; 314-336-1818
E-mail: pphsales@upci.org
Fax: 314-837-6574
Online: www.pentecostalpublishing.com